Palgrave Macmillan Asian Business Series

Series Editor
Yingqi Wei, Business School, University of Leeds, Leeds, UK

The Palgrave Macmillan Asian Business Series publishes theoretical and empirical studies that contribute forward-looking social perspectives on the study of management issues not just in Asia, but by implication elsewhere. The series specifically aims at the development of new frontiers in the scope, themes and methods of business and management studies in Asia, a region which is seen as key to studies of modern management, organization, strategies, human resources and technologies. The series invites practitioners, policy-makers and academic researchers to join us at the cutting edge of constructive perspectives on Asian management, seeking to contribute towards the development of civil societies in Asia and further a field.

Each submission is submitted for single blind peer review. For further information please see our website: https://www.palgrave.com/gp/book-authors/your-career/early-career-researcher-hub/peer-review-process.

To submit a book proposal for inclusion in this series please email Liz Barlow at: liz.barlow@palgrave.com. Details of how to download a proposal form can be found here: https://www.palgrave.com/gp/book-authors/publishing-guidelines/submit-a-proposal.

More information about this series at
http://www.palgrave.com/gp/series/14420

Oliver S. Crocco

Developing Human Resources in Southeast Asia

A Holistic Framework for the ASEAN Community

palgrave
macmillan

Oliver S. Crocco
Louisiana State University
Baton Rouge, LA, USA

ISSN 2661-8435 ISSN 2661-8443 (electronic)
Palgrave Macmillan Asian Business Series
ISBN 978-3-030-79696-9 ISBN 978-3-030-79697-6 (eBook)
https://doi.org/10.1007/978-3-030-79697-6

This Palgrave Macmillan imprint is published by the registered company Springer Nature Switzerland AG
The registered company address is: Gewerbestrasse 11, 6330 Cham, Switzerland

For my partner in life, Khai.

Preface

Studying and writing about ecosystems is a tall task. In general, the process of writing a scholarly book involves parsing out positions and structuring an argument to guide the reader through a set of ideas. This is difficult to do when the phenomenon of interest is an ecosystem, which, by definition, makes sense only via its interconnections and interactions. Like a 5000-piece puzzle, the picture comes alive when the pieces are put together. This is why I believe an ecosystems perspective is so important in understanding Regional Human Resource Development (Regional HRD) because the dimensions shaping the content and processes of HRD in a region make the most sense when viewed together.

How did I come to this work? As an undergraduate, I studied abroad in Turkey and was required to read a variety of books on history, culture, religion, and language. My coursework culminated in a term paper on Islamic mosques, which I presented in the foyer of the Süleymaniye Mosque in Istanbul. We were also required to keep a detailed journal throughout the study abroad experience, which instilled in me the prudent habit of constant reflection and notetaking. This primed me for reflective and curiosity-driven work when I moved to Southeast Asia in 2009. Before beginning my work at Payap University in Chiang Mai, I reached out to a colleague at the university who connected me with a local editor at Silkworm Books who recommended I read David Wyatt's definitive history *Thailand: A Short History*, the novel *Four Reigns* by long-time Thai diplomat Kukrit Pramoj, and *Heartwood of the Bodhi Tree* by

Thai Buddhist philosopher Buddhadāsa Bhikkhu. Like many other non-Thai people fortunate enough to make Thailand their home, I became consumed with Thai history, politics, language, and culture.

After my first two years in the Land of Smiles, I returned to the United States to study Human Development and Psychology at Harvard after which I promptly returned to Payap. As part of my work, I collaborated on a USAID-funded project with the International Rescue Committee to develop three organizational development certificate programs offered to community-based organizations (CBOs) in Myanmar and along the Thailand-Myanmar border. I traveled to dozens of those CBOs and experienced firsthand the power of HRD for individuals, organizations, and communities. Since I was living in Thailand during the frenzy leading up to the implementation of the Association of Southeast Asian Nations (ASEAN) Economic Community in 2015, I began exploring the implications of ASEAN's influence on HRD in the region. I also had the chance to travel to other countries in the region.

These experiences in Southeast Asia deepened my interest in HRD theory, research, and practice and led me to pursue doctoral work in Human and Organizational Learning at the George Washington University. There in Washington, DC, I wrote my first conference paper on HRD in ASEAN in 2016. My dissertation focused on learning, development, and organizational change in Myanmar, and I continued to write and reflect on HRD within the broader regional context. As a faculty member at Louisiana State University, I had the chance to present two additional papers on HRD at the regional level in Southeast Asia at conferences in Bangkok (2018) and Hanoi (2019). I also received a grant in 2019 that allowed me to spend time visiting organizations in the region and at the ASEAN headquarters in Jakarta. The input gained from those conferences and visits with Southeast Asian colleagues and friends proved invaluable to my thought process and mindset. Given the need for regional-level thinking about HRD in Southeast Asia, I took Beverly Cleary's advice, "If you don't see the book you want on the shelves, write it."

To do good scholarship, we must be able to hold paradoxes and complexities with an open hand and not react too hastily to categorize or generalize. Unfortunately, writing a scholarly book such as this takes quite a bit of categorization and generalization. Still, my commitment to my readers is that while I am attempting to synthesize, understand, and articulate the ecosystem of HRD in Southeast Asia, i.e., the processes which the region goes through collectively and individually to enhance the development of its people, it is meant to be held gently. And just as ecosystems themselves are constantly in flux, so this book is meant to be only the beginning of the conversation. In fact, one large purpose of this book is to offer a set of implications for research that might assist other scholars interested in HRD in Southeast Asia given the growing significance of the region.

My positionality as a US-born and US-based researcher is important to note. I am limited by my foreignness to the region despite living and traveling throughout it over the past 12 years. I also recognize the region is generally wary of external influence, which is why one of the key takeaways for me from this writing process has been the importance of elevating and supporting emic perspectives from Southeast Asian scholars. The more conversations I had and the more scholarly books and articles I read, the more I realized how much there is to know given the enormity of the topic. Writing this book has been like pulling at an endless thread of immensely complex social, political, and economic processes. It is truly an interdisciplinary, multidisciplinary, and perhaps transdisciplinary topic. The more I delved into the data related to the Regional HRD ecosystem in Southeast Asia, the more of the story there was to tell. This is just the beginning.

A note on spellings: I tend to be more US-centric, which means I use the term Southeast Asia instead of South East Asia. The name East Timor was primarily used by the Indonesian government during its occupation and is still quite common, but I have opted to use Timor-Leste as it is the preferred name of the Timorese government. I use Lao PDR over Laos, Vietnam over Viet Nam, and Myanmar over Burma. I also tend to avoid using the term "nation" when speaking of Southeast Asian countries given the complex cultural and ethnic diversity and history in the region. Southeast Asia is not ASEAN and vice versa. I typically refer to Southeast Asia as the geographic area, which includes Timor-Leste, and ASEAN in reference to the regional organization, which has yet to admit Timor-Leste as a full member state.

I anticipate a point in need of initial clarification is what HRD is and how it is different from human resource management (HRM). I discuss this in Chapter 1. In short, HRD is more aligned with processes, policies, and activities that facilitate the development of adults' workplace knowledge, skills, mindsets, behaviors, and attitudes. This means it is primarily related to training and development, organization learning and change, career development, and leadership. While there has been considerable concept creep, HRD is different from (or a subset of) the traditional functions of HRM, e.g., compensation and benefits, performance management, and labor relations. Personally, I do not prefer the terminology HRD for its somewhat dehumanizing treatment of humans as "resources" who need to be "developed." It is also slightly outdated at this point and not intuitive for many people outside of academic circles like the Academy of Human Resource Development. However, the idea and verbiage of developing human resources is the language used throughout the governments and regional organization (ASEAN) in Southeast Asia, so I elected to keep it as the primary terminology in this book. I do hope that anyone—scholar, practitioner, student, policymaker—interested in this topic would please reach out and get in touch with me. My foundational belief is that constructing society in a way that empowers people to flourish in relationship with one another and the environment is of utmost importance. I believe Regional HRD can and should be part of this flourishing.

Baton Rouge, USA — Oliver S. Crocco

Acknowledgments

I would like to thank my many friends and colleagues throughout Southeast Asia who inspire me to be the best scholar I can be. It has been an absolute honor to meet and know so many brilliant and passionate people who have informed my thinking on this topic over the years.

I am grateful for regular conversations about Regional Human Resource Development with Oleksandr Tkachenko, Loi Nguyen, and Victoria Jonathan. Thanks to the Academy of Human Resource Development for leading HRD through research and providing me an academic home to interact with thoughtful and critical scholars who have pushed the field forward over the last 28 years. I want to express my deep appreciation for Dean Roland Mitchell of the College of Human Sciences and Education at Louisiana State University for awarding me the Dean's Internationalization Grant that made this book possible. And a special thanks to the most insightful scholar in this field, Maria Cseh of the George Washington University, who has always been there for me and who embodies what it means to be curious. Thanks also to Esther Wakeman for recruiting me to Thailand in the first place and supporting me ever since.

As my first book, I now see how much goes on behind the scenes, so I am grateful for the work of all those at Palgrave Macmillan, especially commissioning editor Marcus Ballenger and Yingqi Wei, editor of the Asian Business Series. Thanks also to Lenna Constantinides who provided piercing feedback and questions on early drafts.

Any task that requires long periods of uninterrupted time to read, reflect, and write involves the immense patience and sacrifice of those closest to us. For me, this has been my wife, Khai. Thanks to her willingness to look after our children, Aden and Alice, I was able to sneak away to my office on Sunday mornings for my most productive writing time of the week. Thanks to my mother for being my first teacher and helping me discover a love of learning; and thanks to my father who taught me to care more about books than cars or clothes. You have played an indescribable role in who I am today.

Contents

Abbreviations

AAC	ASEAN Architect Council
ABD	Asian Development Bank
ACE	ASEAN Confederation of Employers
AEC	ASEAN Economic Community
AFTA	ASEAN Free Trade Area
AFWC	ASEAN Future Workforce Council
ALM	ASEAN Labour Ministers
APEC	Asia-Pacific Economic Cooperation
APFHRM	Asia Pacific Federation of Human Resource Management
AQRF	ASEAN Qualifications Reference Framework
ARPC	Asian Peace and Reconciliation Council
ARQU	Shanghai Ranking Consultancy
ASCC	ASEAN Socio-Cultural Community
ASEAN	Association of Southeast Asian Nations
AsiaDHRRA	Asian Partnership for the Development of Human Resources in Rural Areas
ASPC	ASEAN Political-Security Community
ATA	ASEAN Tourism Agreement
AUN	ASEAN University Network
CBO	Community-Based Organization
CLMV	Cambodia, Lao PDR, Myanmar, and Vietnam
CSO	Civil Society Organization
EDC	Education Development Center
ERIA	Economic Research Institute for ASEAN and East Asia
EU	European Union

FASMEC	Federation of Associations of SME of Cambodia
FDI	Foreign Direct Investment
HDI	Human Development Index
HRD	Human Resource Development
HRM	Human Resource Management
IAI	Initiative for ASEAN Integration
ICT	Information and Communications Technology
IHRD	International Human Resource Development
ILO	International Labor Organization
INGO	International Non-Governmental Organization
IRC	International Rescue Committee
JFC	Jollibee Foods Corporation
Lao PDR	Lao People's Democratic Republic
LSU	Louisiana State University
M&A	Merger and Acquisition
MBNQA	Malcolm Baldrige National Quality Award
MERCOSUR	The Common Market of South America
MIHRM	Malaysian Institute of Human Resource Management
MLQ	Multifactor Leadership Questionnaire
MNC	Multinational Corporation
MOOC	Massive Open Online Courses
MRA	Mutual Recognition Arrangement
MS2W	MekongSkills2Work
MSME	Micro, Small, and Medium Enterprises
NGO	Non-Governmental Organization
NHRD	National Human Resource ddevelopment
NIDA	National Institute for Development Administration
OECD	Organisation for Economic Cooperation and Development
PMAP	Personnel Management Association of Philippines
PMAT	Personnel Management Association of Thailand
PPWSA	Phnom Penh Water Supply Authority
QA	Quality Assurance
R&D	Research and Development
RAVTE	Regional Association of Vocational and Technical Education in Asia
RIHED	Regional Institution for Higher Education and Development
ROK	Republic of Korea
RPO	Rural People's Organization
SADC	South African Development Community
SDG	Sustainable Development Goals
SEAMEO	South-East Asian Ministers of Education Organizations

SEATO	Southeast Asia Treaty Organization
SHRI	Singapore Human Resources Institute
SHRM	Society for Human Resource Management
SLOM	Senior Labour Ministers Meeting
SME	Small- and Medium-Sized Enterprise
SMVTI	Singapore-Myanmar Vocational Training Institute
SOM ED	Senior Officials Meeting on Education
STOU	Sukhothai Thammathirat Open University
TEAM	TVET for ASEAN Mobility
THE	Times Higher Education
ToT	Training of Trainers
TQM	Total Quality Management
TVET	Technical and Vocational Education
UNASUR	Union of South American Nations
UNDP	United Nations Development Programme
USAID	United States Agency for International Development
USAID-LMI COMET	USAID-Lower Mekong Initiative Connecting the Mekong Through Education and Training
USD	United States Dollar (currency)
WB	World Bank

List of Figures

List of Tables

PART I

Researching Human Resource Development in Southeast Asia

CHAPTER 1

Introduction: The Dynamic Region of Southeast Asia

In *Does ASEAN Matter?*, longtime Indonesian diplomat Natalegawa (2018) posed the question, "How can ASEAN become more relevant to the peoples of ASEAN, such that its contributions can be genuinely felt in making better the lives of its citizens?" (p. 1). The short answer put forward in this book is through a collective vision for human resource development (HRD) in the region. While HRD is not an explicit individual pillar of the Association of Southeast Asian Nations (ASEAN), this book shows that there is a complex HRD ecosystem at play in Southeast Asia. Research has been conducted on HRD globally (Marquardt & Engel, 1993; Marquardt et al., 2004), regionally in East Asia (Rasdi & Ismail, 2016), South Asia (Pandey et al., 2016), Sub-Saharan Africa (Nafukho & Muyia, 2016), and nationally in Southeast Asian countries such as Vietnam (Tran et al., 2021), Malaysia and Singapore (Ismail & Rasdi, 2016), and Cambodia (Rana et al., 2017). However, at this point only nascent analyses have been performed to understand HRD at the regional level in Southeast Asia (Crocco et al., 2021; Crocco & Tkachenko, 2018, 2020).

The purpose of this book is to explore and articulate this Regional HRD ecosystem and, in doing so, fuel a robust research agenda and set of contextualized practices for studying and developing human resources in Southeast Asia and ASEAN. This book argues that understanding the

O. S. Crocco, *Developing Human Resources in Southeast Asia*, Palgrave Macmillan Asian Business Series,
https://doi.org/10.1007/978-3-030-79697-6_1

complex ecosystem of Regional HRD in Southeast Asia is a crucial step for scholars, practitioners, policymakers, and students to comprehend and then make contributions toward the collective flourishing of Southeast Asian citizens. Before unpacking the Regional HRD ecosystem in Southeast Asia, it is worth becoming familiar with the region of Southeast Asia, the regional organization of ASEAN, and the defining characteristic of ASEAN, i.e., the ASEAN Way.

1.1 The Region of Southeast Asia

Is Southeast Asia a region? The consensus among scholars, practitioners, and international organizations like the United Nations (2019) is that Southeast Asia includes the 11 countries of Brunei Darussalam, Cambodia, Indonesia, the Lao People's Democratic Republic (PDR), Malaysia, Myanmar, the Philippines, Singapore, Thailand, Timor-Leste (commonly referred to as East Timor), and Vietnam. The consideration of Southeast Asia as a quasi-unified region dates back to academic writing in the 1920s (Croissant & Lorenz, 2018) and then in more general use in the 1940s as a convenient wartime grouping (Beng, 2014). The term Southeast Asia later became reinforced with the establishment of the Southeast Asia Treaty Organization (SEATO) in 1954 (Emmerson, 1984). Then, it was with the founding of ASEAN in 1967 by its initial five member states (Indonesia, Malaysia, the Philippines, Singapore, and Thailand), that the status of "functional regionalism" was introduced, which transcended regionalism based on geography alone (Weatherbee, 2019, p. 2). As ASEAN continued to welcome additional members in subsequent years (i.e., Brunei, Cambodia, Lao PDR, Myanmar, Vietnam) and strengthen relations with external partners (e.g., China, Japan, South Korea), its operative principle of "open regionalism" became more visible (Akrasanee, 2015, p. 15). Open regionalism "seeks to promote economic integration amongst participants without discrimination against other economies" which allowed ASEAN and individual member states to cooperate with countries around the world openly (Drysdale & Vines, 1998, p. 103).

This iterative establishment of a regional identity supports the idea of a region as an "imagined community" (Smouts, 1998, p. 22) which acknowledges the subjective construction of a regional identity via "symbolic representations" (p. 27). In this type of regionalism, names like Southeast Asia simultaneously "describe and invent reality" (Emmerson,

1984, p. 1). As a result of ASEAN's increasing visibility and activity, ASEAN itself is often conflated with Southeast Asia (e.g., Thangavelu & Chongvilaivan, 2013), ignoring the presence of Timor-Leste, which became an independent country in 2002 and is currently not a member of ASEAN despite ongoing deliberations on its candidacy (Berlie, 2018). While this book considers the development of human resources in South east Asia as a whole, it focuses primarily on the 10 member countries of ASEAN with additional discussion about Timor-Leste's role in the Regional HRD ecosystem.

Together, the 11 countries of Southeast Asia represent remarkable diversity in terms of politics and geography (see Table 1.1), culture (see Table 1.2), and economics (see Table 1.3). The region includes Indonesia, which is the fourth most populous country in the world with close to half a billion people, as well as Brunei, with fewer than half a million (see Table 1.1). And the region is only expected to grow both in population and in human development, according to the East–West Center (2002), with an estimated population in Southeast Asia in 2050 of 800,302,000 and an estimated life expectancy of 77.3 years. This diversity is also seen in the fact that Indonesia, Myanmar, and Thailand each span over 500,000 km^2 of land and sea, while Brunei, Timor-Leste, and Singapore combined cover less than 25,000 km^2. The region also exhibits political diversity, as represented by one-party socialist republics (Vietnam and Lao PDR), constitutional monarchies (Cambodia and Thailand), and constitutional republics (Philippines and Singapore). The region has also seen the rise of military juntas with Thailand (2014) and Myanmar (2021) as recent examples. With the exception of Malaysia, which has a federal system, all Southeast Asian countries are unitary states meaning that the national government has authority over the other political subdivisions.

In Southeast Asia, there are strong religious loyalties at work (see Table 1.2), which can bring about circumstances, as in the case of Indonesia, where "the nation-state no longer has the exclusive monopoly of the loyalty of its people" (Natalegawa, 2018, p. 12). The residents of Southeast Asia practice a variety of major religions such as Islam (Brunei, Indonesia, Malaysia), Christianity (Philippines, Timor-Leste), Buddhism (Cambodia, Lao PDR, Myanmar, Thailand, Singapore), and secularism or no affiliation (Vietnam). It should be noted, however, that data on religious affiliation in Southeast Asia often does not account for the syncretism of belief systems, local practices, and folk religions that can skew statistics. For example, Swearer (2010) shows how Buddhism in

Table 1.1 Examples of political and geographic diversity

Country	*Population (thousands; 2019)*	*Land Area (sq. km; 2018)*	*Political systems*
Brunei	433.29	5,270	Unitary Islamic absolute monarchy
Cambodia	16,4866486.54	176,520	Unitary dominant-party parliamentary elective constitutional monarchy
Indonesia	270,625.57	1,877,519	Unitary presidential constitutional republic
Lao PDR	7169.45	230,800	Unitary Marxist-Leninist one-party socialist republic
Malaysia	31,949.78	328,550	Federal parliamentary constitutional elective monarchy
Myanmar	54,045.42	652,790	Unitary parliamentary assembly-independent republic (currently under a military junta as of March 2021)
Philippines	108,116.62	298,170	Unitary presidential constitutional republic
Singapore	5703.57	709	Unitary dominant-party parliamentary constitutional republic
Thailand	69,625.58	510,890	Unitary parliamentary constitutional monarchy
Timor-Leste	1293.12	14,870	Unitary semi-presidential constitutional republic
Vietnam	96,462.11	310,070	Unitary Marxist-Leninist one-party socialist republic

Source World Bank (n.d.), Croissant and Lorenz (2018), and Wikipedia (n.d.)
Note According to its constitution, Brunei is a hereditary constitutional monarchy; however, given the Sultan's absolute sovereignty and separation from the government, it is more accurately described as an absolute monarchy (Croissant & Lorenz, 2018)

Table 1.2 Examples of cultural diversity

Country	*Religion (% of population)*	*Official languages*	*Education (mean years of schooling)*	*Human Development Index (rank)*
Brunei	Muslim (78.8%)	Malay (Bahasa Melayu)	9.1	0.838 (47)
Cambodia	Buddhist (96.3%)	Khmer	5	0.594 (144)
Indonesia	Muslim (87.2%)	Bahasa Indonesia	8.2	0.718 (107)
Lao PDR	Buddhist (64.7%)	Lao	5.3	0.613 (137)
Malaysia	Muslim (61.3%)	Bahasa Malaysia	10.4	0.810 (62)
Myanmar	Buddhist (87.9%)	Burmese	5	0.583 (147)
Philippines	Roman Catholic (80.2%)	Filipino (Tagalog) and English	9.4	0.718 (107)
Singapore	Buddhist (33.2%)	English, Mandarin, Malay, and Tamil	11.6	0.938 (11)
Thailand	Buddhist (94.6%)	Thai	7.9	0.777 (79)
Timor-Leste	Roman Catholic (97.6%)	Tetun Prasa and Portugese	4.8	0.606 (141)
Vietnam	No affiliation (81.8%)	Vietnamese	8.3	0.704 (117)

Sources CIA (n.d.) and United Nations Development Programme (2020)

Southeast Asia has melded with local folk traditions over time. In terms of language, no two Southeast Asian countries share the same official language except for the Philippines and Singapore where English is one of the multiple official languages.

Consider also assessments of development such as the human development index (HDI), which measures and ranks countries according to their health, education, and standard of living (UNDP, n.d.). Southeast Asia includes countries like Myanmar, which was named "Least Developed Country" in 1987 (United Nations, 2016) and still has the lowest HDI score of the ASEAN Member States (see Table 1.3). In contrast, Southeast Asia also includes countries like Singapore, with life expectancy of 83 years and an HDI often among the top ten countries in the world. While the vast majority of Southeast Asian countries have adult literacy rates over 95%, countries like Cambodia, Myanmar, and Lao PDR have

Table 1.3 Examples of economic diversity

Country	*Labor force (thousands; 2020)*	*GDP (millions: USD; 2019)*	*GDP per capita (USD; 2019)*	*Global Competitiveness Rank (score)*	*World Bank Atlas Status (2021)*
Brunei	216.69	13,469.42	31,086.8	56 (62.8)	High income
Cambodia	9,163.34	27,089.39	1,643.1	106 (52.1)	Lower-middle income
Indonesia	134,615.73	1,119,190.78	4,135.6	50 (64.6)	Upper-middle income
Lao PDR	3,828.61	18,173.84	2,534.9	113 (50.1)	Lower-middle income
Malaysia	15,904.36	364,681.37	11,414.2	27 (74.6)	Upper-middle income
Myanmar	22,951.39	76,085.85	1,407.8	–	Lower-middle income
Philippines	43,719.20	376,795.51	3,485.1	64 (61.9)	Lower-middle income
Singapore	3,511.95	372,062.53	65,233.3	1 (84.4)	High income
Thailand	38,483.13	543,548.97	7,806.7	40 (68.1)	Upper-middle income
Timor-Leste	559.60	2,017.92	1,560.5	-	Lower-middle income
Vietnam	56,542.50	261,921.24	2,715.3	67 (61.5)	Lower-middle income

Sources World Bank (n.d.), World Bank (2021), and World Economic Forum (2019a)

rates that hover meagerly around 85% (ASEAN, 2020). There are also gender disparities within countries such as Lao PDR's female adult literacy rate being only 62.9% in 2017 (ASEAN, 2020). That said, every Southeast Asian country has improved its HDI score over the past decade (2010 and 2019) (ASEAN, 2020), which reflects regional, national, and organizational efforts to improve development in the region.

There is also incredible diversity regionally in terms of economics (see Table 1.3). The region has Singapore with a GDP per capita of 65,233 USD on par with the United States and Qatar among the highest in the world and three countries with GDP per capita under 2,000 USD (Cambodia, Myanmar, and Timor-Leste). The region includes countries with massive labor forces, like Indonesia with 134 million and Vietnam with 56 million alongside small labor forces, like Brunei and Timor-Leste with less than one million combined. Given that eight out of 11

Southeast Asian countries hover around middle income according to the World Bank's Atlas Method, HRD becomes increasingly important as it relates to moving out of middle-income status. In their research on "overcoming the middle-income trap" in ASEAN member countries, Hardiana and Hastiadi (2019) argue that innovation through investments in research and development, training, and education is the best mechanism for moving into high-income status. Once these investments are made, through government funding as well as foreign direct investment, "labor quality must be refined toward high-skill intensive labors and productivity must be intensified to enable growth in the industrial sector" (Hardiana & Hastiadi, 2019, p. 60).

Similarly, the extent to which Southeast Asian countries can harness the power of HRD is key for regional integration and regional competitiveness (Sakane et al., 2018). Competitiveness, according to the World Economic Forum (2019b) is defined as "the set of institutions, policies and factors that determine the level of productivity of a country" (para 4). According to the World Economic Forum's (2019a) Global Competitiveness Index of 141 countries, Southeast Asia as a region includes the top-ranked country in the world (Singapore) as well as the 106th ranked country (Cambodia) and the 113th ranked country (Lao PDR) (see Table 1.3). HRD policy and practice alongside institutional adoption and support of HRD are vital components to competitiveness in this sense.

Despite this multifaceted diversity across a range of political, cultural, and economic factors, these countries have sought to create regional stability and economic prosperity through a regional organization. Much of the motivation for regional collaboration came in response to centuries-long colonization, the vast majority of which ended in the mid-twentieth century. While Thailand was never officially colonized due to a strong monarchy and the fact that it served as a buffer between colonial powers, the Philippines was colonized by the United States until 1946, Indonesia was colonized by the Netherlands until 1949, and Malaysia and Singapore were colonized by the British until 1957 and 1965 respectively (Croissant & Lorenz, 2018). Before ASEAN was founded, several earlier attempts at a regional organization had failed, such as the Association of Southeast Asia in 1961, made up of Thailand, the Philippines, and Malaysia (Wilson, 1964), and the organization MAPHILINDO in 1963, which, as its name suggests, was founded by Malaysia, the Philippines, and Indonesia (Jackson et al., 1986). Thanks largely to the perseverance and vision of Thai foreign minister Thanat Khoman and Indonesian minister of foreign affairs Adam Malik, a lasting regional organization became a reality in 1967 with ASEAN by the founding members of Indonesia, Malaysia, the Philippines, Singapore, and Thailand. In a way, it was Thanat Khoman's unique positionality as a representative of Thailand, which had, that allowed him to navigate the intraregional tensions at that time and draft the first declaration that became ASEAN's founding document: The Bangkok Declaration (ASEAN, 1967; Irvine, 1982). This gave Southeast Asia a "regional consciousness" that would evolve over time into a unique regional organization (Khoman, 1968), one that is still evolving to this day.

1.2 The Regional Organization of ASEAN

While the original objectives of ASEAN related to the prevention of internal armed conflict and foreign subjugation (Severino, 2015), the vision continued to develop and expand. In 1976, the Treaty for Amity and Cooperation brought about a commitment to economic integration, which included the countries supporting one another with "training and research facilities in the social, cultural, technical, scientific, and administrative fields" (ASEAN, 1976a). Regional cooperation was moved further front and center with the establishment of the ASEAN Free Trade Area (AFTA) in 1992 (Fry, 2008), which motivated governments to support the development of human resources. During this time, ASEAN membership grew to include Brunei (1984), Vietnam (1995), Lao PDR (1997), Myanmar (1997), and Cambodia (1999).

ASEAN exemplifies the type of regional integration that encompasses multidimensionality, going beyond economics and including "dimensions of politics, diplomacy, security, culture, etc." (Lombaerde & Langenhove, 2006, p. 9). In 2003, the vision for a grouping of countries into more than just an association but rather one ASEAN Community was established with the ASEAN Charter (2008). The ASEAN Charter marked a major turning point in bringing about regional integration across three distinct but overlapping communities: the ASEAN Political-Security Community (APSC), the ASEAN Socio-Cultural Community (ASCC), and the ASEAN Economic Community (AEC). Guided by Community Blueprints (i.e., strategic plans), these three communities are made up of a total of 43 sectoral ministerial bodies (see Table 1.4), which delegate

Table 1.4 ASEAN sectoral ministerial bodies

Community	*Sectoral ministerial body*
ASEAN Political-Security Community	ASEAN Foreign Ministers Meeting
	Commission on the Southeast Asia Nuclear Weapon-Free Zone
	ASEAN Defence Ministers Meeting
	ASEAN Law Ministers Meeting
	ASEAN Ministers/Attorneys-General Meeting of the Central Authorities on Mutual Legal Assistance in Criminal Matters
	ASEAN Ministerial Meeting on Transnational Crime
	ASEAN Ministerial Meeting on Drug Matters
	ASEAN Regional Forum
ASEAN Economic Community	ASEAN Economic Ministers Meeting
	ASEAN Free Trade Area Council
	ASEAN Investment Area Council
	ASEAN Finance Ministers Meeting
	ASEAN Central Bank Governors Meeting
	ASEAN Finance Ministers and Central Bank Governors Meeting
	ASEAN Ministers Meeting on Agriculture and Forestry
	ASEAN Ministers on Energy Meeting
	ASEAN Ministerial Meeting on Minerals
	ASEAN Ministerial Meeting on Science, Technology and Innovation
	ASEAN Digital Ministers Meeting
	ASEAN Transport Ministers Meeting
	Meeting of the ASEAN Tourism Ministers
	ASEAN Mekong Basin Development Cooperation
	ASEAN Centre for Enter
	ASEAN-Japan Centre in Tokyo
ASEAN Socio-Cultural Community	ASEAN Ministers Responsible for Information
	ASEAN Ministers Responsible for Culture and Arts
	ASEAN Education Ministers Meeting
	ASEAN Ministerial Meeting on Disaster Management

(continued)

Table 1.4 (continued)

Community	*Sectoral ministerial body*
	ASEAN Ministerial Meeting on the Environment Conference of the Parties to the ASEAN Agreement on Transboundary Haze Pollution ASEAN Health Ministers Meeting ASEAN Labour Ministers Meeting ASEAN Ministers on Rural Development and Poverty Eradication ASEAN Ministerial Meeting on Women ASEAN Ministerial Meeting on Social Welfare and Development ASEAN Ministerial Meeting on Youth Heads of Civil Service Meeting for the ASEAN Cooperation on Civil Service Matters ASEAN Ministerial Meeting on Sports ASEAN Centre for Biodiversity ASEAN Coordinating Centre for Humanitarian Assistance on Disaster Management ASEAN Earthquakes Information Centre ASEAN Specialized Meteorological Centre ASEAN University Network

Source ASEAN (2019)

responsibilities for carrying out the vision of the ASEAN Charter. Leadership of the regional organization is shared among member states with the Chairmanship of ASEAN rotating annually between the member states in alphabetical order and holding two annual ASEAN Summits.

In addition to supporting political security, ASEAN has played a key role in attracting international attention, respectability, and foreign direct investment. One of the biggest changes in the last 50 years in Southeast Asia has been the shift from a "trust-deficit to strategic trust" (Natalegawa, 2018, p. 14). In a region riddled with conflicting interests and reeling from colonial rule, there had been immense distrust between Southeast Asian countries, and ASEAN began a trust-building process towards collective goals for political security. As the countries continued to work together strategically, a host of issues related to regional integration emerged such as labor migration, tourism, and Mekong River flows, which have required regional solutions. When the headquarters of

ASEAN, the ASEAN Secretariat, was established in 1981, it was agreed that all members would contribute equal shares to fund it (ASEAN, 1976b), which represents the way that ASEAN elevates shared leadership, equality, and harmony. As a result, however, ASEAN's overall operational budget remains low because of the inability of low-income countries like Lao PDR and Myanmar to offer extensive funding (Destradi, 2020). This limited budget is also one of the drivers for seeking external funding from extra-regional partners like the United States and China as well as from organizations like the European Union (EU).

Despite its initial priority of regional security, ASEAN is not only concerned with intraregional affairs; it is constantly engaged in partnership with other nations. It has established bilateral agreements with its dialogue partners (e.g., India, United States) and special arrangements such as the ASEAN + Three Cooperation, which includes summits, agreements, and collaborative initiatives with China, Japan, and South Korea. This latter arrangement is especially important considering the geopolitical quandaries of some Southeast Asian member states such as Myanmar, which is wedged between China and India (Myint-U, 2012), and Vietnam and the "East Sea". In a lecture at Yale in 2019, Singaporean Ambassador Bilahari Kausikan shared a story in which he asked a Vietnamese foreign minister about the relationship between Vietnam and China. The foreign minister responded, "Every Vietnamese leader... must be able to get along with China. Every Vietnamese leader must be able to stand up to China. And if you don't think you can do both at the same time, you do not deserve to be a leader" (Kausikan, 2019).

While this book takes the position that ASEAN is indeed a significant actor in Southeast Asia, it is important to note that its efficacy and strength as a regional organization lie not in its ability to mandate and control but rather to facilitate. The real players are the individual member states, not the association (Weatherbee, 2019). Thus, to ascribe the economic output of the combined member states to ASEAN would be equivalent to giving ASEAN the credit for the region's cultural diversity.

Regional integration as a phenomenon is not limited to Southeast Asia; it is found in other multi-country collaborative endeavors such as the EU, the Union of South American Nations (UNASUR), and the South African Development Community (SADC). These organizations differ from ASEAN in important ways. For example, ASEAN diverges from the EU in its ambitions, perspectives of economic integration, political norms, and norm diffusion (Allison, 2015). ASEAN member states also do not share the same general liberal democratic political values that EU member countries generally espouse (Acharya, 2001). While the EU has enacted a common budget and currency along with other norms of economic integration, ASEAN has approached economic integration more slowly and has avoided a common currency (Allison, 2015). According to Gungwu (2015), "ASEAN is entirely strategic" (p. 8). As a result, much to the frustration of some onlookers, it ends up emphasizing processes over outcomes (Allison, 2015). Yet, in a comparative multi-case study of regional organizations in the Global South, Krapohl (2017) found ASEAN to be the most successful in terms of regional integration. When compared to SADC in South Africa and the Common Market of South America (MERCOSUR), ASEAN was most successful for its ability to avoid intraregional conflict and maintain fruitful extra-regional relationships. As Tan Sri Datuk Dr. Rebecca Fatima Sta. Maria (2018) of the Economic Research Institute for ASEAN and East Asia (ERIA) points out, ASEAN's integration was not modeled after the EU or any other regional block. It was very much an inductive process that allowed ASEAN values to emerge. The core of these values, which separates ASEAN from other regional organizations, is what is called *the ASEAN Way* (Destradi, 2020).

1.3 The ASEAN Way

Built into ASEAN since its founding is a set of guiding principles, which has morphed into a collective mindset known as the ASEAN Way. The phrase itself is thought to have first been used by an Indonesian general in 1975 (Acharya, 1998), but the principles behind the phrase were articulated clearly in the Bangkok Declaration (ASEAN, 1967) and further laid out in the Treaty for Amity and Cooperation in 1976:

a. Mutual respect for the independence, sovereignty, equality, territorial integrity and national identity of all nations;
b. The right of every State to lead its national existence free from external interference, subversion or coercion;
c. Non-interference in the internal affairs of one another;
d. Settlement of differences or disputes by peaceful means;
e. Renunciation of the threat or use of force;
f. Effective cooperation among themselves (ASEAN, 1976a).

The core principles of the ASEAN Way are ***musjawarah***, the concept of deliberation, and ***mufakat***, decision-making via consensus, which Indonesia's first president, Sukarno, brought to the fore in Southeast Asian politics (Weatherbee, 2019). In practice, the ASEAN Way amounts to "informality, preference for consensus over majority voting, avoidance of legalistic procedures, preference for non-binding resolutions, and a tendency to avoid contentious bilateral issues in multilateral discussions" (Acharya, 2018, p. 89). The ASEAN Way exemplifies the fact that ASEAN is not a rule-based, outcomes-oriented organization but rather a strategic endeavor that values relationships, balance, and gradual change. As a result, ASEAN moves at the speed of the comfort level of its members.

The principles laid out in the Treaty for Amity and Cooperation in 1976 and the subsequent principles espoused in the ASEAN Charter in 2008 mark only the formal components of the ASEAN Way. Ongoing processes of "interaction, socialization, compromise and adjustment" have continued to influence the ASEAN Way as an institution in the region (Acharya, 1998, p. 57). The ASEAN Way is a continuous "process of identity building" (Acharya, 2001, p. 29) and the lifeblood of what makes ASEAN a "socially constructed reality" (Abad, 2007). The power of the ASEAN Way to transcend the cultural, political, and economic diversity of its member countries and minimize internal conflicts represents a substantial and enduring achievement, what some have termed a miracle (Mahbubani & Sng, 2017). The ASEAN Way has allowed for ***unity and diversity*** among its member states, which is especially important as the focus of ASEAN has shifted from primarily security concerns to ***people-centered***, both common slogans. ASEAN's increasing focus on the well-being of its people is further evidence of the recognized need to develop the human resources of the region.

1.4 Human Resource Development

Developing human resources, also known as human resource development (HRD), describes the processes, policies, and activities that coordinate the development of knowledge, skills, competencies, and mindsets of adults in the workplace (McGuire, 2014). HRD is both a profession carried out in organizations and a field of study that is built on the foundation of related fields such as management, psychology, sociology, anthropology, education, economics, and philosophy (Chalofsky, 2014).

In what has become a widely used and cited definition of the concept, McLean and McLean (2001) describe HRD as follows:

> any process or activity that, either initially or over the long term, has the potential to develop adults' work-based knowledge, expertise, productivity and satisfaction, whether for personal or group/team gain, or for the benefit of an organization, community, nation, or ultimately, the whole of humanity. (p. 322)

While there is some overlap between HRD and its conceptual cousin, human resource management (HRM) (Ruona & Gibson, 2004), HRD focuses more on training, learning, performance, and leadership in organizations. In contrast, HRM tends to emphasize personnel functions in organizations, compliance, and payroll. HRD is also different from comparable terms such as human capital development, which emphasizes the role of K-12 schooling and healthcare and is related more closely with associating a monetary value of people (Becker, 1993). Still, the recognition in Human Capital Theory "that peoples' learning capabilities are of comparable value to other resources involved in the production of goods and services" makes it related to HRD and thus included in the analysis of this study (Nafukho et al., 2004, pp. 545–546).

Much to the irritation of some scholars in HRD and related fields, HRD remains capacious and in a state of continual change and emergence (Lee, 2010, 2016). HRD can be understood and analyzed at the individual, organizational, community, national, regional, and global levels (Lynham & Cunningham, 2006). While the word "regional" is also a subcategory of national and was used in this sense by Ahn and McLean (2008) in their study on competencies in southeast Korea, this book focuses on HRD at the regional level in terms of geographic region including multiple countries. Thus, Regional HRD relies heavily on the idea of National HRD (NHRD) (McLean, 2006), which can be understood as.

> an undertaking at the top level of government and throughout the country's society that coordinates all activities related to human development (HD) to create greater efficiency, effectiveness, competitiveness, satisfaction, productivity, knowledge, spirituality, and well-being of its residents. It includes education, health, safety, training, economic development, culture, science and technology, and any factors influencing HD. (slide 19, as cited in McLean, 2014)

Considering the cross-country differences in national strategies (or lack thereof) for developing human resources, there are various expressions of NHRD around the world. Cho and McLean (2004) identified five different models of NHRD, including a centralized model (e.g., China), a transitional model (e.g., South Korea), a "government-initiated model toward standardization" (p. 384) (e.g., United Kingdom), a decentralized model (e.g., Canada), and a small-nation model (e.g., St. Lucia). In their analysis of the NHRD strategies of India and China, Alagaraja and Wang (2012) synthesize NHRD models into nine overlapping factors that influence NHRD in different country contexts including education systems, the role of government in establishing national skill frameworks, the relationship between industry needs and skill development, and cultural influences on training systems. Garavan et al. (2018) have provided a multi-level analysis of NHRD to show that these systems of developing human resources within a national context exist within the greater global context of global standards and regulations, the global economy, and global migration. The literature shows a clear jump between individual countries and how they develop their human resources and the global context. While Lynham and Cunningham (2006) mention a regional level, they provide no additional analysis, and the idea of region as a collection of countries is absent from McLean and McLean's (2001) definition. This absence is where this book comes in.

1.5 Regional Human Resource Development in Southeast Asia

Building off nascent existing literature on Regional HRD, this study analyzes the Regional HRD ecosystem in the case of Southeast Asia and ASEAN. A preliminary definition describes the concept of Regional HRD as "a collective vision with corresponding activities for human resource development carried out by a group of countries for the benefit of their individuals, organizations, communities, nations, and the region as a whole" (Crocco & Tkachenko, 2020). Within the context of Southeast Asia, the primary facilitator of Regional HRD is ASEAN. HRD and related concepts such as human capital development, workforce development, and talent development are central to the vision of the ASEAN community and are referenced thousands of times in official ASEAN publications. In the context of ASEAN, Regional HRD includes processes and activities at three overlapping and intersecting levels. First,

ASEAN exists as a coordinating and facilitating organization in the region. Second, Regional HRD exists as the combined NHRD of the ten member states of ASEAN and Timor-Leste. While each country in Southeast Asia develops its labor force according to its own implicit or explicit NHRD strategy, each country's NHRD affects and is affected by Southeast Asia's Regional HRD. Lastly, Regional HRD exists in relationship with extra-regional partners such as China, Japan, and South Korea, which make up the aforementioned ASEAN + Three Collaboration and work collaboratively on a host of HRD and HRD-related projects in the region.

Since its founding, ASEAN has initiated a variety of policies and activities related to the enhancement and development of its workforce including the establishment of the ASEAN Economic Community, which seeks to make Southeast Asia a single market and production base with a free flow of skilled labor within the region (ASEAN, 2015a, 2015b). While the three ASEAN communities are separate, they are seen as mutually reinforcing. For example, even before the ASEAN Charter of 2008, the Declaration of ASEAN Concord II (Bali Concord II) of 2003, professed a clear call for HRD under the ASEAN Socio-Cultural Community in relationship with the region's economic goals:

> ASEAN shall ensure that its work force shall be prepared for, and benefit from, economic integration by investing more resources for basic and higher education, training, science and technology development, job creation, and social protection. The development and enhancement of human resources is a key strategy for employment generation, alleviating poverty and socio-economic disparities, and ensuring economic growth with equity. ASEAN shall continue existing efforts to promote regional mobility and mutual recognition of professional credentials, talents, and skills development. (ASEAN, 2003, para 18)

Given the interrelationships between HRD and other aspects of the region such as poverty alleviation and workforce mobility, understanding how human resources are being developed in the region and contributing to a vibrant regional workforce in Southeast Asia has never been more pressing.

Despite the size and growing presence of Southeast Asia, there is little representation of Southeast Asian countries in HRD and HRD-related journals. Southeast Asia consistently receives less attention in the management and education literature (Barrot, 2021; Rowley & Warner, 2007). Moreover, just as the field of Southeast Asian studies has been "dominated by empirical studies on individual communities, villages, towns and nation-states" (Evers, 1999, p. 414), so research on HRD in Southeast Asia has been located within individual organizations and countries thus lacking macro perspectives. In books on global HRD like Marquardt and Engel (1993), Southeast Asian countries are lumped together with East Asia and given little special attention. This neglect shows that further research is needed.

Understanding HRD at the regional level in Southeast Asia is significant for several overarching reasons. The ten member states of ASEAN have decided to work together for the betterment of their citizens. This decision has tied their fates together, especially when considering the ASEAN Economic Community. The four pillars of the ASEAN Economic Community include (1) the free flow of goods, services, and investments and the mostly free flow of capital; (2) a competitive regional economic policy, e.g., infrastructure and intellectual property rights; (3) equitable economic development; and (4) integration into the global economy. HRD plays a key role in, and is influenced by, these pillars. For example, information and communications technology (ICT) has played an important role in Southeast Asia's development as a region, yet it is HRD "that drives technological change and international competitiveness" in the region (Rasia, 2002, p. 108). One persistent challenge in the region related to HRD has been addressing the ASEAN Development Gap between the CLMV countries (i.e., Cambodia, Lao PDR, Myanmar, and Vietnam) and the remaining six countries (McGillivray et al., 2013). This is played out in a variety of areas such as logistics development and service liberalization where a country like Cambodia needs to work with its neighbors Thailand and Vietnam on issues such as cross-border trade (Chheang, 2017). In this case and many others like it, HRD holds the key to policy implementation and closing development gaps between neighboring countries. However, in a study of challenges facing ASEAN member countries, human capital development broadly conceived was the top challenge identified by seven ASEAN member countries (Asian Development Bank Institute, 2016).

We also know that HRD is an important mechanism for drawing foreign direct investment (FDI) (McGuire, 2014) and thus predates the ASEAN Economic Community. As Irawati and Rutten (2014) show,

Southeast Asian countries, in particular the "ASEAN-5" i.e., Indonesia, Malaysia, the Philippines, Singapore, and Thailand are attractive to multinationals and FDI for their wealth of human resources. In May 2000, in the wake of the 1997 Asian Financial Crisis, the ASEAN Labor Ministers met and agreed on the Vision and Mission Statements that would promote "the full potential and dignity of workers and address changes in the labour market arising from the forces of globalization, trade liberalization and economic integration" (ASEAN, 2001, p. vii). Even before the 1997 financial crisis, initiatives like the Human Resource Development Fund in Singapore and Malaysia as well as Singapore's Skills Development Fund were used to develop skills in the workforce and relieve any potential negative impacts on the labor force as the result of crises. HRD and a skilled labor force, even more than the availability of cheap labor, is what draws FDI to Southeast Asia (Hoang & Bui, 2015). And FDI has increased in the region over the past decade. Inward flows of FDI to ASEAN countries from other ASEAN countries have increased from 15.5 million USD in 2010 to 22 million USD in 2019 (ASEAN, 2020). FDI has also increased from the rest of the world into ASEAN countries from 92.9 million USD in 2010 to 136.8 million USD in 2019 (ASEAN, 2020).

HRD in ASEAN is more than just skill development; it is connected to other dimensions of well-being. ASEAN (2001) states that "investments in appropriate training to increase employability [should] be accompanied by measures to ensure that decent working conditions are brought about, since productivity, creativity, as well as innovation—requires a sense of freedom, dignity, and equality at the workplace" (p. 37). In his 2017 Keynote Address at the ASEAN-China-UNDP Symposium on Financing the Implementation of the SDGs in ASEAN, Dr. Surakiart Sathirathai, Former Deputy Prime Minister and Minister of Foreign Affairs of Thailand and Chairman of the Asian Peace and Reconciliation Council (APRC), said the following:

> Success in developing the human resources has proved to be the key component to sustainable development in every ASEAN Member State. That is why the Leaders of ASEAN, through the ASEAN Charter, set out the purposes of ASEAN in particular to develop human resources through closer cooperation in education and life-long learning, in science and technology, for the empowerment of the peoples of ASEAN and for strengthening of the ASEAN Community. (ASEAN, 2017, p. 6)

In this sense, HRD is connected to more than merely economic considerations, extending to the sustainability of the region and the "ethical and moral commitment to human flourishing" found at the nexus of human development and HRD (Kuchinke, 2010, p. 575). For example, in the ASEAN Socio-Cultural Community (ASCC), HRD plays an important role in supporting rural development and poverty eradication (Anggo & Laja, 2018). The numerous motivations for and applications of HRD in the region, as well as the different actors and drivers of HRD across the 10 member countries of ASEAN and Timor-Leste, result in a high degree of complexity, which requires an equally complex framework to comprehend.

1.6 An Ecosystems Perspective: Shaping a Region's Human Resource Development

This study applies an ecosystems perspective of HRD (Garavan et al., 2019) to the Southeast Asian region and argues that viewing HRD in Southeast Asia as a complex adaptive system is the most effective way to understand the expansive and multifarious processes and activities involved in Regional HRD. A complex adaptive system can be understood generally as "a collection of individual agents with freedom to act in ways that are not always totally predictable, and whose actions are interconnected so that one agent's actions changes the context for other agents. Examples include the immune system, a colony of termites, the financial market, and just about any collections of humans" (Plsek & Greenhalgh, 2001, p. 625).

An ecosystems perspective as it relates to HRD provides a way of understanding "the multiplicity of actors that work collaboratively to shape IHRD [International HRD] practices, develop IHRD systems, and add value to individuals, organizations, countries, regions, and society" (Garavan et al., 2019, p. 249). An ecosystems perspective of IHRD asserts that HRD does not simply consist of isolated activities occurring in insulated organizations (Garavan et al., 2019). Rather, IHRD is a spectrum of interconnected and overlapping dimensions that are mutually constituting and mutually influencing. Garavan et al. (2019) separate these content dimensions into a macro-level (e.g., government support, culture, global talent mobility), meso-level (e.g., professional HRD networks, educational institutions, networks), and microlevel (e.g., employees, workers, and firms).

As the world becomes increasingly interconnected and networked, centralized or simplistic approaches to understanding complex phenomena like Regional HRD are less reflective of reality (Scharmer & Kaufer, 2013). While texts like Yaw et al.'s (2000) study of Indonesia, Malaysia, and Singapore provided an important introduction to the complexities inherent in developing human resources in Southeast Asia, to date, little research exists which seeks to analyze the region as a whole. Using an ecosystems framework, this study applies the content and process dimensions outlined by Garavan et al. (2019) within the context of Regional HRD in Southeast Asia (see Fig. 1.1). The Regional HRD ecosystem is situated within the larger IHRD ecosystem, which is seen, for example, in the transfer of HRD-related practices from countries like Germany to subsidiaries in Singapore, Thailand, and Indonesia (Stehle & Erwee, 2007). While discussing international influences, this study primarily focuses on the Regional HRD ecosystem and delves less into the extra-regional influences of which more is discussed by Crocco and Tkachenko (2020).

While not comprehensively studied, there is some precedent that HRD functions as an ecosystem in the regional context of Southeast Asia. In

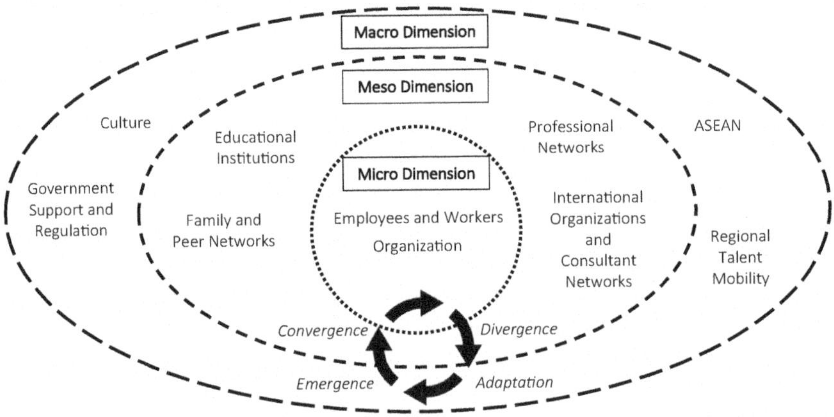

Fig. 1.1 The regional HRD ecosystem of Southeast Asia (*Note* All content and process dimensions of the Regional HRD ecosystem in Southeast Asia are constantly influenced by political, economic, social, technological, environmental, and legal forces)

2005, Brunei hosted a convention entitled "HR Challenges & Opportunities in the New Economy" where over 20 scholars presented papers related to HRD in the region, which was subsequently published by Metusin and Beng (2005) in the book "HRD for developing states and companies." One of the papers presented at the convention and then published in the book was by longtime HRD scholar and political scientist, Chartchai Na Chiangmai of the National Institute of Development Administration in Thailand who spoke about the "ecology" of HRD in the region. While his chapter centers organizations in this ecology, he writes that both public and private sector organizations in Southeast Asia must develop their capabilities to "(1) conceive and execute complex strategies; (2) acquire, share, and protect intellectual capital, particularly indigenous wisdom; and (3) manage the interaction of networks of interests and forces in society to the best benefit of the organization and those in the ecology" (Chiangmai, 2005, p. 35).

An ecosystems approach helps to address some of the disconnect that other approaches tend to have. Scharmer and Kaufer (2013) talk about a set of disconnects in our current economic landscape that an ecosystems perspective helps remedy. These include, for example, the disconnect between those in leadership positions and their followers as well as those in power and the many disenfranchised (Scharmer & Kaufer, 2013). Responding to the dramatic technological, organizational, political, and environmental changes will require a systemic perspective that identifies the interrelationships across dimensions and actors (Scharmer & Kaufer, 2013).

In addition to the ecosystems perspective, this study is informed by macro perspectives on HRD such as International HRD (Wang & McLean, 2007), Global HRD (Garavan et al., 2016), National HRD (McLean, 2014; Oh et al., 2013), and the emerging concept of Regional HRD (Crocco & Tkachenko, 2018, 2020; Crocco et al., 2021). This book presents a holistic framework for Regional HRD in Southeast Asia and ASEAN, which is presented initially here in this chapter (see Fig. 1.1) and then further expounded upon in subsequent chapters.

1.7 Structure of the Book

To present the analysis of Regional HRD from an ecosystems perspective, Chapter 2 outlines the research design of the study, which includes the data sources, data collection methods, and data analysis methods informing the study. Then, the book discusses the major content dimensions that make up the Regional HRD ecosystem in Southeast Asia. These include the macro dimension of culture, policy, and ASEAN (Chapter 3); the meso dimension of education and professional and family networks (Chapter 4); and the micro dimension of employees, workers, and organizations (Chapter 5). Chapter 6 considers the process dimension of the Regional HRD ecosystem in Southeast Asia by focusing on the processes of emergence, convergence, divergence, and continuous adaptation within ASEAN. Chapter 6 combines the aforementioned content and process dimensions and returns to the holistic framework for the ASEAN Community presented here. The book concludes with Chapter 7, in which the future of HRD in Southeast Asia is discussed, critiques of and questions about the Regional HRD perspective are highlighted, and implications for HRD research, policy, and practice are articulated.

Bibliography

Abad, M. C. (2007). *Constructing the social ASEAN*. Available at https://asean.org/?static_post=constructing-the-social-asean-m-c-abad-jr.

Acharya, A. (1998). The 'ASEAN way' and regional order. *Contemporary Security Policy, 19*(1), 55–84.

Acharya, A. (2001). *Constructing a security community in Southeast Asia: ASEAN and the problem of regional order.* Routledge.

Acharya, A. (2018). *Constructing global order: Agency and change in world politics.* Cambridge University Press.

Ahn, Y., & McLean, G. N. (2008). Competencies for port and logistics personnel: An application of regional human resource development. *Asia Pacific Education Review, 9*(4), 542–551.

Akrasanee, N. (2015). The evolving nature of ASEAN's economic cooperation: Original vision and current practice. In O. K. Beng, S. B. Das, T. Chong, M. Cook, C. Lee, & M. Yeo, *The 3rd ASEAN reader* (pp. 14–16). ISEAS Publishing.

Alagaraja, M., & Wang, J. (2012). Development of a national HRD strategy model: Cases of India and China. *Human Resource Development Review, 11*(4), 407–429. https://doi.org/10.1177/1534484312446190.

Allison, L. (2015). *The EU, ASEAN and interregionalism: Regionalism support and norm diffusion between the EU and ASEAN*. Palgrave Macmillan.

Anggo, F. A., & Laja, L. (2018). ASEAN socio-cultural community: ASEAN approach and effort in rural development and poverty eradication. *SHS Web of Conferences, 53*(01004), 1–5. https://doi.org/10.1051/shsconf/201853 01004.

Asian Development Bank Institute. (2016). *ASEAN 2030: Toward a borderless economic community*. Brookings Institution Press.

Association of Southeast Asian Nations. (1967). *The Bangkok declaration*. https://asean.org/the-asean-declaration-bangkok-declaration-bangkok-8-august-1967/.

Association of Southeast Asian Nations. (1976a). *Treaty of amity and cooperation in Southeast Asia*. https://asean.org/treaty-amity-cooperation-southeast-asia-indonesia-24-february-1976/.

Association of Southeast Asian Nations. (1976b). *Agreement on the establishment of the ASEAN Secretariat*. https://asean.org/?static_post=asean-secretariat-basic-documents-agreement-on-the-establishment-of-the-asean-secretariat-bali-24-february-1976-2.

Association of Southeast Asian Nations. (2001). *Preparing workers for changes in the labour market: The ASEAN experience*. ASEAN Secretariat.

Association of Southeast Asian Nations. (2003). *Declaration of ASEAN Concord II (Bali Concord II)*. https://asean.org/?static_post=declaration-of-asean-concord-ii-bali-concord-ii.

Association of Southeast Asian Nations. (2015a). *Kuala Lumpur declaration on the establishment of the ASEAN community*. https://www.asean.org/wp-content/uploads/2015/12/KL-Declaration-on-Establishment-of-ASEAN-Community-2015.pdf.

Association of Southeast Asian Nations. (2015b). *ASEAN Economic Community Blueprint 2025*. https://www.asean.org/storage/2016/03/AECBP_2025r_FINAL.pdf.

Association of Southeast Asian Nations. (2017). *Keynote address by Professor Dr. Surakiart Sathirathai at ASEAN-China-UNDP symposium on financing the implementation of SDGs in ASEAN*. https://asean.org/wp-content/uploads/2017/08/Keynote-Address-By-Professor-Dr.-Surakiart-Sathirathai-Former-Deputy-Prime-Minister-and-Minister-of-Foreign-Affairs-of-Thailand-Chairman-of-Asian-Peace-and-Reconciliation-Council-APRC.pdf.

Association of Southeast Asian Nations. (2019). *ASEAN sectoral ministerial bodies*. https://asean.org/asean/asean-structure/asean-sectoral-ministerial-bodies/.

Association of Southeast Asian Nations. (2020). *ASEAN statistical yearbook 2020*. https://www.aseanstats.org/wp-content/uploads/2020/12/ASYB_2020.pdf

Barrot, J. S. (2021). Research on education in Southeast Asia (1996–2019): A bibliometric review. *Educational Review*. https://doi.org/10.1080/00131911.2021.1907313.

Becker, G. (1993). *Human capital: A theoretical and empirical analysis with special reference to education* (3rd ed.). University of Chicago Press.

Beng, O. K. (2014). *The Eurasian core and its edges: Dialogues with Wang Gungwu on the history of the world*. ISEAS Publishing.
Berlie, J. A. (2018). *East Timor's independence, Indonesia, and ASEAN*. Palgrave Macmillan.
Central Intelligence Agency. (n.d.). *The World Factbook—East Asia/Southeast Asia*. https://www.cia.gov/the-world-factbook/east-asia-southeast-asia/.
Chalofsky, N. (2014). Introduction: The profession and the discipline. In N. E. Chalofskky, T. S. Rocco, & M. L. Morris (Eds.), *Handbook of human resource development* (pp. xxxvii–lv). Wiley.
Chheang, V. (2017). FDI, services liberalization and logistics development in Cambodia. In T. S. Yean & S. Basu Das (Eds.), *Services liberalization in ASEAN* (pp. 268–296). Palgrave Macmillan.
Chiangmai, C. N. (2005). Human-focused management for future progress. In A. G. Metusin & O. K. Beng (Eds.), *HRD for developing states and companies: Proceedings of the 2005 Brunei Darussalam AEMC convention* (pp. 32–46). Institute for Southeast Asian Studies.
Cho, E., & McLean, G. N. (2004). What we discovered about NHRD and what it means for HRD. *Advances in Developing Human Resources, 6*(3), 382–393. https://doi.org/10.1177/1523422304266090.
Crocco, O. S., & Tkachenko, O. (2018, November 8–10). *Human resource development in ASEAN: Are we ready to discuss the concept of Regional Human Resource Development?* [presentation]. The 17th International Asian Conference of the Academy of Human Resource Development, Bangkok, Thailand.
Crocco, O. S., & Tkachenko, O. (2020). Regional human resource development: The case of Southeast Asia and ASEAN. *Human Resource Development International*. https://doi.org/10.1080/13678868.2020.1858261.
Crocco, O. S., Nguyen, L., & Tkachenko, O. (2021). Vietnam and regional human resource development in ASEAN. In H. T. Tran, T. T. Phuong, H. T. M. Van, & G. N. McLean (Eds.), *Human resource development in Vietnam: Research and practice* (pp. 97–117). Palgrave Macmillan. https://doi.org/10.1007/978-3-030-51533-1_4.
Croissant, A., & Lorenz, P. (2018). *Comparative politics of Southeast Asia: An introduction to governments and political regimes*. Springer.
Debrah, W. A., McGovern, I., & Budhwar, P. (2000). Complementarity or competition: The development of human resources in a South-East Asian growth triangle: Indonesia, Malaysia and Singapore. *International Journal of Human Resource Management, 11*(2), 314–335. https://doi.org/10.1080/095851900339891.
Destradi, S. (2020). The finances of the Association of Southeast Asian Nations (ASEAN). In U. Engel & F. Mattheis (Eds.), *The finances of regional organizations in the Global South* (pp. 206–220). Routledge.

Drysdale, P., & Vines, D. (Eds.). (1998). *Europe, East Asia and APEC: A shared global agenda?* Cambridge University Press.

East-West Center. (2002). *The future of population in Asia*. East-West Center.

Emmerson, D. K. (1984). "Southeast Asia": What's in a name? *Journal of Southeast Asian Studies, 15*(1), 1–21. https://doi.org/10.1017/S0022463400012182.

Evers, H. (1999). Review of reconceptualizing Southeast Asia. *International Quarterly for Asian Studies, 30*(3–4), 414.

Fry, G. (2008). *The Association of Southeast Asian Nations*. Infobase Publishing.

Garavan, T., McCarthy, A., & Carbery, R. (2019). An ecosystems perspective on international human resource development: A meta-synthesis of the literature. *Human Resource Development Review, 18*(2), 248–288. https://doi.org/10.1177/1534484319828865.

Garavan, T., McCarthy, A., & Morley, M. (2016). Global human resource development: Landscaping the anatomy of an evolving field. In T. Garavan, A. McCarthy, & M. Morley (Eds.), *Global human resource development: Regional and country perspectives* (pp. 1–16). Routledge.

Garavan, T., Wang, J., Matthews-Smith, G., Nagarathnam, B., & Lai, Y. (2018). Advancing national human resource development research: Suggestions for multilevel investigations. *Human Resource Development International, 21*(4), 288–318. https://doi.org/10.1080/13678868.2018.1429171.

Gungwu, W. (2015). Southeast Asia and foreign empires. In O. K. Beng, S. B. Das, T. Chong, M. Cook, C. Lee, & M. Yeo (Eds.) *The 3rd ASEAN reader* (pp. 5–8). ISEAS Publishing.

Hardiana, S. N., & Hastiadi, F. F. (2019). Overcoming the middle-income trap: The role of innovation on switching onto a higher income group for ASEAN member states. In F. F. Hastiadi (Ed.), *Globalization, productivity and production networks in ASEAN* (pp. 57–86). Palgrave Macmillan.

Hoang, H. H., & Bui, D. H. (2015). Determinants of foreign direct investment in ASEAN: A panel approach. *Management Science Letters, 5*, 213–222. https://doi.org/10.5267/j.msl.2014.12.015.

Irawati, D., & Rutten, R. (Eds.). (2014). *Emerging knowledge economies in Asia: Current trends in ASEAN 5*. Routledge.

Irvine, R. (1982). The formative years of ASEAN: 1967–1975. In A. Broinowski (Ed.), *Understanding ASEAN* (pp. 8–36). Macmillan Press.

Ismail, M., & Rasdi, R. M. (2016). Human resource development in Malaysia and Singapore. In T. N. Garavan, A. M. McCarthy, & M. J. Morley (Eds.), *Global human resource development: Regional and country perspectives* (pp. 104–127). Routledge.

Jackson, K. D., Paribatra, S., & Djiwandono, J. S. (Eds.). (1986). *ASEAN in regional and global context*. Institute of East Asian Studies.

Kausikan, B. (2019, September 30). *How to think about Southeast Asia.* Yale University. https://www.youtube.com/watch?v=IXfGY1an9jQ.

Khoman, T. (1968, June 25). Opening address at the Inaugural Session of the ASEAN Ad Hoc Committee on Civil Aviation at the Ministry of Foreign Affairs, Bangkok.

Krapohl, S. (Ed.). (2017). *Regional integration in the global south.* Palgrave Macmillan.

Kuchinke, K. P. (2010). Human development as a central goal for human resource development. *Human Resource Development International, 13*(5), 575–585. https://doi.org/10.1080/13678868.2010.520482.

Lee, M. (2010). Shifting boundaries: The role of HRD in a changing world. *Advances in Developing Human Resources, 12*(5), 524–535.

Lee, M. (2016). *On the nature of human resource development: Holistic agency and an almost-autoethnographical exploration of becoming.* Routledge.

Lombaerde, P. D., & Langenhove, L. V. (2006). Indicators of regional integration: Conceptual and methodological aspects. In P. D. Lombaerde (Ed.), *Assessment and measurement of regional integration* (pp. 9–41). Routledge.

Lynham, S. A., & Cunningham, P. W. (2006). National human resource development in transitioning societies in the developing world: Concept and challenges. *Advances in Developing Human Resources, 8*(1), 116–135. https://doi.org/10.1177/1523422305283150.

Mahbubani, K., & Sng, J. (2017). *The ASEAN miracle: A catalyst for peace.* National University of Singapore Press.

Maria, R. F. S. (2018, January 22). *ASEAN economic integration: Myth or reality.* Lee Kuan Yew School of Public Policy. https://www.youtube.com/watch?v=QD7TNPkeaRY.

Marquardt, M., Berger, N., & Loan, P. (2004). *HRD in the age of globalization.* Basic Books.

Marquardt, M., & Engel, D. (1993). *Global human resource development.* Prentice Hall.

McGillivray, M., Feeny, S., & Iamsiraroj, S. (2013). Understanding the ASEAN development gap. In M. McGillivray & D. Carpenter (Eds.), *Narrowing the development gap in ASEAN: Drivers and policy options* (pp. 21–64). Routledge.

McGuire, D. (2014). *Human resource development* (2nd ed.). Sage.

McLean, G. N. (2006). *Human capital theories and practices: Gaining a competitive advantage through national HRD* [presentation]. Junkasem University and Ratchapat Universities, Thailand.

McLean, G. N. (2014). National HRD. In N. E. Chalofsky, T. S. Rocco, & M. L. Morris (Eds.), *Handbook of human resource development* (pp. 643–660). Wiley .

McLean, G. N., & McLean, L. (2001). If we can't define HRD in one country, how can we define it in an international context? *Human Resource Development International, 4*(3), 313–326.

Metusin, A. G., & Beng, O. K. (2005). *HRD for developing states and companies: Proceedings of the 2005 Brunei Darussalam AEMC convention*. Institute for Southeast Asian Studies.

Myint U, T. (2012). *Where China meets India: Burma and the new crossroads of Asia*. Farrar, Straus, and Giroux.

Nafukho, F. M., Hairston, N. R., & Brooks, K. (2004). Human capital theory: Implications for human resource development. *Human Resource Development International, 7*(4), 545–551. https://doi.org/10.1080/1367886042000299843.

Nafukho, F. M., & Muyia, H. M. A. (2016). Human resource development in Sub-Saharan Africa. In T. N. Garavan, A. M. McCarthy, & M. J. Morley (Eds.), *Global human resource development: Regional and country perspectives* (pp. 131–147). Routledge.

Natalegawa, M. (2018). *Does ASEAN matter?* ISEAS Publishing.

Oh, H., Choi, Y., & Choi, M. (2013). Comparative analysis of OECD member countries' competitive advantage in National Human Resource Development system. *Asia Pacific Education Review, 14*(2), 189–208.

Pandey, S., Hewapathirana, G. I., & Pestonjee, D. M. (2016). Human resource development in South Asia. In T. N. Garavan, A. M. McCarthy, & M. J. Morley (Eds.), *Global human resource development: Regional and country perspectives* (pp. 63–85). Routledge.

Plsek, P., & Greenhalgh, T. (2001). The challenge of complexity in health care. *British Medical Journal, 323*(7313), 625–628. https://doi.org/10.1136/bmj.323.7313.625.

Raharso, A., & Goh, M. (2014). Regional headquarters in ASEAN: Do they add or destroy value? In. D. Irawati & R. Rutten (eds.), *Emerging knowledge economies in Asia: Current trends in ASEAN 5* (pp. 13–34). Routledge.

Rana, S., Ardichvili, A., & Taing, S. K. (2017). National human resource development in a transitioning society: The case of Cambodia. *Human Resource Development International, 20*(2), 127–146. https://doi.org/10.1080/13678868.2016.1243937.

Rasdi, R. M., & Ismail, M. (2016). Human resource development in East Asia. In T. N. Garavan, A. M. McCarthy, & M. J. Morley (Eds.), *Global human resource development: Regional and country perspectives* (pp. 39–62). Routledge.

Rasia, R. (2002). Human capital and IT in innovation and growth in ASEAN. In C. S. Yue & J. J. Lim (Eds.), *Information technology in Asia: New development paradigms* (pp. 83–110). Institute of Southeast Asian Studies.

Rowley, C., & Warner, M. (2007). Business and management in South East Asia: Studies in diversity and dynamism. In C. Rowley & M. Warner (Eds.), *Management in South-East Asia: Business culture, enterprises, and human resources* (pp. 1–13). Routledge.

Ruona, W. E., & Gibson, S. K. (2004). The making of twenty-first-century HR: An analysis of the convergence of HRM, HRD, and OD. *Human Resource Management, 43*(1), 49–66.

Sakane, K., & JICA Study Team on ASEAN 2025 Report. (2018). ASEAN integration: Opportunities and challenges. In K. Kobayashi, K. A. Rashid, M. Furuichi, & W. P. Anderson (Eds.), *Economic integration and regional development: The ASEAN economic community* (pp. 11–33). Routledge.

Scharmer, C. O., & Kaufer, K. (2013). *Leading from the emerging future: From ego-system to eco-system economies.* Barrett-Koehler Publishers, Inc.

Severino, R. C. (2015). From political/security concerns to regional economic integration. In O. K. Beng, S. B. Das, T. Chong, M. Cook, C. Lee, & M. Yeo (Eds.), *The 3rd ASEAN reader* (pp. 17–22). ISEAS Publishing.

Smouts, M. (1998). The region as the new imagined community? In P. Le Galès & C. Lequesne (Eds.), *Regions in Europe: The paradox of power* (pp. 22–28). Routledge.

Stehle, W., & Erwee, R. (2007). Transfer of human resource practices from German multinational enterprises to Asian subsidiaries. *Research and Practice in Human Resource Management, 15*(1), 63–88.

Swearer, D. K. (2010). *The Buddhist world of Southeast Asia* (2nd ed.). State University of New York Press.

Thangavelu, S., & Chongvilaivan, A. (2013). *Globalization, outsourcing, and labor development in ASEAN*. Routledge.

Tran, H. T., Phuong, T. T., Van, H. T. M., & McLean, G. N. (Eds.). (2021). *Human resource development in Vietnam: Research and practice.* Springer Nature.

United Nations. (2016). *List of least developed countries.* http://www.un.org/en/development/desa/policy/cdp/ldc/ldc_list.pdf.

United Nations. (2019). *International Migration 2019.* https://www.un.org/development/desa/pd/sites/www.un.org.development.desa.pd/files/files/documents/2020/Jun/international_migration_2019_report_june20.pdf.

United Nations Development Programme. (n.d.). *Human Development Index.* http://hdr.undp.org/en/content/human-development-index-hdi.

United Nations Development Programme. (2020). *Human Development Reports.* http://hdr.undp.org/en.

Wikipedia. (n.d.). *Southeast Asia.* https://en.wikipedia.org/wiki/Southeast_Asia.

World Bank. (n.d.). *World Bank open data.* https://data.worldbank.org.

World Bank. (2021). *World Bank Country and Lending Groups*. https://datahelpdesk.worldbank.org/knowledgebase/articles/906519-world-bank-country-and-lending-groups.

World Economic Forum. (2019a). *The global competitiveness report 2019*. http://www3.weforum.org/docs/WEF_TheGlobalCompetitivenessReport2019.pdf.

World Economic Forum. (2019b). *Global Competitiveness Report 2019: How to end a lost decade of productivity growth*. https://www.weforum.org/reports/how-to-end-a-decade-of-lost-productivity-growth.

Weatherbee, D. E. (2019). *ASEAN's half century: A political history of the Association of Southeast Asian Nations*. Rowman & Littlefield.

Wilson, D. A. (1964). Thailand: A new leader. *Asian Survey, 4*(2), 711–715. https://www.jstor.org/stable/3023579.

Yaw, D. A., McGovern, I., & Budhwar, P. (2000). Complementarity or competition: The development of human resources in a South-East Asian Growth Triangle: Indonesia, Malaysia, and Singapore. *International Journal of Human Resource Management, 11*(2), 314–335.

Yeates, N. (2019). World regional social governance, policy and development. In J. Midgley, R. Surender, & L. Alfers (Eds.), *Handbook of social policy and development* (pp. 224–245). Edward Elgar Publishing Ltd.

CHAPTER 2

Research Design

2.1 Research Framework

The research design for this study relies on various types of literature review and content analysis to examine a broad range of sources related to Regional HRD in Southeast Asia. The study does not attempt to test a specific theory but rather explore and develop theory. Thus, it does not employ a strictly a priori strategy but begins by exploring and applying the framework of an ecosystems perspective of HRD (Garavan et al., 2019) while remaining open to uncovering other components that emerge within the context of Southeast Asia. As a result, it incorporates literature based in a broad range of theoretical frameworks that function within the knowledge domain of HRD.

The philosophical orientation of this study relies on critical realism (Bhaskar, 1978), which accepts the realist position in terms of ontology but embraces relativism and the role of social and historical conditioning in terms of epistemology (Mingers, 2014). In other words, critical realism recognizes that actors and structures exist in a way that leads to actual events (realism), while at the same recognizing that all perceptions of those structures and events are viewed through the lens of individuals whose culture and history influence their perceptions. The purpose of critical realism is to explain a phenomenon by focusing on the structures and mechanisms at play. Critical realism encompasses "retroduction," which

O. S. Crocco, *Developing Human Resources in Southeast Asia*, Palgrave Macmillan Asian Business Series,
https://doi.org/10.1007/978-3-030-79697-6_2

"involves imagining a model of a mechanism, which, if it were real, would account for the phenomenon in question" (Bhaksar, 2014, p. vii). Critical realism has been applied to organizational research (Edwards et al., 2014) with the central goal to "synthesize from the available ideas and relevant data an account of what is happening to key social mechanisms and processes" (Ackroyd & Karlsson, 2014, p. 21). Thus, while this study seeks to describe existing literature and documents, it also attempts to discover the underlying mechanisms that facilitate and operate in the Regional HRD ecosystem.

This study is particularly well-suited for a critical realist approach because it relies on a certain level of "eclecticism and creativity" (Ackroyd & Karlsson, 2014, p. 22). It takes an extensive approach to data collection from a wide variety of sources to understand the context and mechanisms operating within the Regional HRD ecosystem. While some go so far as to call ASEAN a miracle (Mahbubani & Sng, 2017) and others critique its every move (and lack of movement) (see Chapter 7), this book takes a more middle-of-the-road approach. Rather than make a direct value judgment or criticism, it seeks primarily to understand and describe. That said, as mentioned in the foreword, the positionality of the researcher is never fully bracketed from the analysis.

2.1.1 Research Questions

In the planning stage for this study, an advisory group (Briner & Denyer, 2012) of HRD scholars and practitioners with experience in Southeast Asia was consulted. The group helped hone the focus of the study to arrive at two main research questions.

RQ1: How do scholarly literature, ASEAN documents, government reports, and white papers describe the components and structure of the Regional HRD ecosystem in Southeast Asia?

RQ2: How do these components inform a holistic framework for understanding the Regional HRD ecosystem in Southeast Asia?

2.1.2 Methodology

Investigating a phenomenon as multifaceted, complex, and broad as a Regional HRD ecosystem requires a comprehensive methodological approach. Therefore, this study combines methodological techniques from several approaches: integrative literature review (Torraco, 2005, 2016), systematic literature review (Briner & Denyer, 2012), and qualitative meta-synthesis (Sandelowski & Barroso, 2007).

The methodology for this study reflects many of the characteristics of an integrative literature review, which "reviews, critiques, and synthesizes representative literature on a topic in an integrated way" (Torraco, 2005, p. 356). Torraco (2005) discusses two reasons for an integrative literature review: (1) to review an established topic in the field that needs synthesizing as a way to develop new conceptualizations, make connections and classifications within the literature, and participate in new theorizing; and (2) to review the literature on a new and emerging topic to bring together loose ends, establish the significance of the topic for the field, and pave the way forward. In many ways, the use of integrative literature review in this study is driven by both reasons. For one, regional cooperation in Southeast Asia, which involves issues related to HRD such as labor migration and skill development has long been studied in the fields of political science, economics, and sociology. In that sense, this study is building upon and synthesizing a vast body of literature. More accurately, however, this study is driven by the second reason for conducting an integrative literature review in that the concept of Regional HRD is relatively new (Crocco & Tkachenko, 2020; Crocco, et al., 2021). Not only is the concept new, but very little research has also explored the phenomenon within the context of Southeast Asia.

The methodological approach for this study also borrows techniques from systematic literature review, which is typically applied to quantitative research synthesis (Briner & Denyer, 2012; Tranfield et al., 2003). The study seeks to employ a process that is, to a degree, "replicable, scientific and transparent" (Tranfield et al., 2003, p. 209), in which the structure is derived from the research questions. The systematic literature review process involves identifying relevant sources, appraising the sources, analyzing the findings, and synthesizing the findings to reveal new knowledge accessible to both scholars and practitioners (Briner & Denyer, 2012).

The methodological approach for this study is also guided by the principles of meta-synthesis (Sandelowski & Barroso, 2007). Specifically, this study privileges the synthesis and integration of the disparate sources over comparison and critique. It also fosters an explicit understanding of the different purposes, positionalities, and representations within and across various data sources. Concerning the synthesis of the literature, in particular, a configurative approach is adopted, in which the researcher seeks to understand a phenomenon by "interpreting and arranging (configuring) information" as well as "identifying patterns provided by heterogeneity" (Gough et al., 2012, pp. 3–4). While the study reviews the literature and documents within a set of guidelines and structures, the latter have been adjusted throughout the iterative process of research and writing.

2.2 Data Sources and Collection

Given the broad and diverse scope of this study, data were selected from eight distinct categories of sources. Those categories include scholarly literature; ASEAN publications; ASEAN statements, communiques, and press releases; ASEAN Summit documents; other ASEAN publications; newspapers and magazines; government reports and documents; and white papers and reports from international organizations and non-governmental organizations (NGOs) functioning within Southeast Asia. First, these sources are described and then the data collection and analysis processes are explained.

2.2.1 *Scholarly Literature*

A wide range of peer-reviewed academic journal articles, scholarly book chapters, and scholarly books formed the foundation of the analysis. While each piece of scholarly literature was assessed for its contribution to understanding the phenomenon in question, a wide net was cast to understand the breadth of the available literature. Therefore, not only international databases such as ProQuest and Business Source Complete but also other scholarly sources were searched and included. As of January 1, 2021, 499 total publications were reviewed.

2.2.2 *ASEAN Publications*

ASEAN publications are official ASEAN documents on a variety of topics including annual reports, project overviews, policies, strategic plans, and reports. These were collected to understand official ASEAN policies and projects related to Regional HRD. All publications available on the ASEAN website were downloaded for review. As of January 1, 2021, 372 total publications were reviewed.

2.2.3 *ASEAN Statements, Communiques, Press Releases*

ASEAN statements, communiques, and press releases were also collected. These documents range from brief 100–200 word to 5–6-page documents and cover a wide range of topics related to ASEAN. Specifically, they illuminate official ASEAN positions, programs, and current events as they relate to Regional HRD. All of the documents available were downloaded for review. As of January 1, 2021, 3787 total statements, communiques, and press releases were reviewed.

2.2.4 *ASEAN Summit Documents*

ASEAN Summits are the official meetings of ASEAN leaders. The first ASEAN Summit was held in 1976; since 2009, the summits have been held biannually. Each ASEAN Summit produces a set of press releases, speeches, declarations, and agreements. As of January 1, 2021, 483 were reviewed.

2.2.5 *Other ASEAN Documents*

ASEAN produces a variety of other noteworthy documents that includes speeches and statements by ASEAN Secretaries-General and Deputy Secretaries-General, selected commentary by other leaders within and beyond the region such as ASEAN Member State prime ministers/presidents (487 total reviewed as of January 1, 2021), a collection of opinion pieces and editorials in various newspapers around the world (52 total reviewed as of January 1, 2021), and a collection of white papers presented at various conferences and meetings by ASEAN representatives (49 total reviewed as of January 1, 2021). These documents provide additional important information regarding Regional HRD, such as the perspectives of leaders and representatives of ASEAN and the degree to which they discuss components of the Regional HRD ecosystem.

2.2.6 *Newspapers and Magazines*

This study also relied on newspapers and magazines to clarify commentary and details related to the HRD ecosystem that might not appear in the scholarly literature or ASEAN documents. Recently, Southeast Asia and ASEAN have received more attention in the media; however, as former

Secretary-General of ASEAN Rodolfo C. Severino pointed out in 1999, that was not the case in the first 31 years of ASEAN's existence (Severino, 1999). Major English-language newspapers in each of the 11 Southeast Asian countries (e.g., *Bangkok Post*, *Strait Times*) were included in this study, along with magazines focusing on Southeast Asian issues (e.g., *Southeast Asia Globe*).

2.2.7 Government Reports

The official governmental websites, documents, and reports of all of the Southeast Asian countries also provided an important source of data for the study. In particular, statements, publications, and policies related to HRD and related issues were identified, focusing on areas such as labor, workforce development, and higher education. This also includes official statistics and data, keeping in mind that data quality in Southeast Asia exists on several tiers (Stagers, 2016).

2.2.8 White Papers

White papers from international organizations and NGOs within and beyond the region formed the final set of data for the study. This category includes reports such as The Asia Foundation's "The Future of Work Across ASEAN" (Karr et al., 2020) and books such as the Asian Development Bank's *Skilled Labor Mobility and Migration: Challenges and Opportunities for the ASEAN Economic Community* (Gentile, 2019).

2.3 Data Collection

To understand Regional HRD in Southeast Asia from an ecosystems perspective, one of the following HRD-related terms was paired with one of the following context terms in searches across the data sources:

> <u>HRD-related search terms</u>: human resource(s) development, HRD, human resource(s) management, HRM, human resource(s), skill(s) development, workforce, talent, labor, human capital development, vocational education, training, capacity building
> <u>Contextual search terms</u>: Southeast Asia, South East Asia, ASEAN, Brunei Darussalam, Cambodia, Indonesia, Lao PDR, Malaysia,

Myanmar, Philippines, Singapore, Timor-Leste, Thailand, and Vietnam.

Both British and American spellings were utilized in the searches (e.g., "labor" and "labour") and additional iterations were searched such as Brunei, Viet Nam, Laos, and Burma. Short or differently spelled adjectival forms of country names were also searched, such as Thai, Burmese, Malay, and Laotian. These search terms were developed based on initial explorations of this topic by Crocco et al. (2021) and Crocco and Tkachenko (2020) along with assistance from advisors.

2.3.1 *Scholarly Literature Search*

The search of the scholarly literature was based on the following criteria: (a) sources must address an area of the International HRD (IHRD) ecosystems perspective in one or more of the 11 countries in Southeast Asia; (b) sources must be published in a peer-reviewed journal or scholarly book; and, (c) sources must be published in the English language. To maintain the depth of the research while acknowledging that cultural, political, and economic realities shift over time, no date range was imposed. Each structured search in the aforementioned databases was a Boolean search consisting of paired HRD-related and contextual (e.g., Southeast Asia or Malaysia) terms. To be considered for review, articles had to have at least one reference to HRD or an HRD-related search term in the title and/or abstract and one contextual search term in the title/and/or abstract. Articles were screened according to the criteria with particular attention paid to ensuring that HRD policy, practice, or research was addressed.

First, a general search was conducted using the Boolean search term combinations at Louisiana State University's (LSU) libraries using the "Discovery" collection of 315 databases, which contains over 10,000 journals including Academic Search Complete, Bibliography of Asian Studies, Business Source Complete, ERIC, Human Resources Abstracts, JSTOR, Professional Development Collection, PsycARTICLES, PsycINFO, SAGE Journals Online, ScienceDirect, SocINDEX, SpringerLink, Web of Science, and Wiley Online Library. Limiting the search to this collection of databases would have biased the results toward publications in international journals; thus, searches of Google Scholar, researchgate.net, academia.edu, and other online sources were also conducted. In addition, various searches were made of Southeast Asian university-based journals such as the *Asian Pacific Migration Journal* and *ASEAN Journal of Community Engagement*. These journals, which were suggested by advisors and/or additional searches, are not cataloged in large international databases such as ProQuest. The search also included the proceedings of relevant conferences such as the Academy of Human Resource Development, which holds annual conferences in the Americas, Asia, and Europe.

2.3.2 Other Data Sources Search

All official ASEAN data sources were downloaded from www.asean.org except for some official ASEAN documents, which were only available through a third-party document hosting site. Newspapers and magazine articles were accessed and searched using a combination of LSU Libraries and individual sites. Government reports and documents were accessed at the official government websites of the 11 countries in Southeast Asia. White papers and reports of international organizations and NGOs were accessed via the individual organizations. The latter were identified through keyword searches and in discussions with advisors. In all cases, if a source referenced another source that appeared to be relevant to the research questions, that source was also located and screened for inclusion in the study.

2.4 Data Analysis

All data sources were screened for their connection to the HRD-related search terms and context terms. Instances of search pairs were then reviewed according to their relevance to Regional HRD and the components and processes of an international HRD ecosystems perspective according to Garavan et al. (2019). Sources were excluded if the connection between the HRD-related search term and the contextual search term was only tangential or if no conceptual connection was made between the HRD-related search term and the contextual search term.

This scholarly search resulted in a data set of 499 articles, book chapters, and books that included search pairs, e.g., human resources + the Philippines, human resource development + ASEAN, labor mobility + Southeast Asia, etc. After screening, a total of 278 sources informed the study. The search of the other data sources resulted in a total of 438 sources that included at least one HRD-related search term and one contextual search term, which informed the analysis.

2.4.1 Coding

All data sources were coded using a modified inductive approach based on Garavan et al.'s (2019) ecosystem perspective of IHRD. Descriptive codes were derived from the sources, focusing on the main areas of the Regional HRD ecosystem (e.g., macro, meso, and micro dimensions) These codes were then grouped into categories. This process was supported by several members of the advisory group to ensure accurate coding of the data sources.

2.4.2 Analysis

The data were analyzed using qualitative content analysis (Hsieh & Shannon, 2005) and thematic analysis (Joffe & Yardley, 2004; Ryan & Bernard, 2003) techniques. The qualitative content analysis relied on a summative approach, which began by "identifying and quantifying certain words or content in text with the purpose of understanding the contextual use of the words or content" (p. 1283). In this study, the content analysis focused on HRD and HRD-related terms and the components and processes of an HRD ecosystem. Additional dimensions not mentioned by Garavan et al. (2019) were also explored such as the influence of a regional organization. For the thematic analysis, salient sections within the sources relating to Regional HRD were organized according to emergent themes (Joffe & Yardley, 2004; Ryan & Bernard, 2003). These themes were then used to describe the Regional HRD ecosystem in Southeast Asia and to develop the holistic framework.

2.5 Advantages and Limitations

The methodological approach used in this study has several advantages and limitations. First, the approach is advantageous in that it facilitated the collection of literature on a topic that has received little scholarly focus, i.e., Regional HRD in Southeast Asia. A second but related advantage of the approach is that its use allowed for as broad and as all-encompassing a search for related data sources as possible. To date, no one has brought together such a vast amount of data on this topic and sought to make sense of Regional HRD in this manner. In this sense, it serves as an important starting point for future scholars interested in the topic and its many dimensions. As additional literature and data emerge, the searches in this study can be refined, allowing future researchers to contribute new and different conceptualizations.

Despite these advantages, the approach also has several limitations. First, when data are drawn from as broad a scope as possible, important sources and contributions are inevitably missed. This limitation was especially pertinent in this study, considering the inclusion criterion of English language sources. Despite English being the official language of ASEAN (Crocco & Bunwirat, 2014), excellent scholarly contributions have been made in languages other than English. Second, even though a largely replicable and transparent process was used to collect and review the data sources, advisors and colleagues would occasionally mention a source that might not otherwise appear in a search. Additionally, sources referred to by other sources might lead to areas that did not appear elsewhere for any number of reasons. There are also many articles, sources, and stories worth exploring in more depth in the book but were not included due to time or space constraints.

Lastly, this book analyzes the data sources according to a certain philosophical orientation and theoretical perspective. As such, other approaches are necessarily excluded or not primarily discussed. For example, this book employs an ecosystems perspective. While it discusses institutional theory (Rattanasevee, 2014), particularly when discussing the macro dimension, an exclusively institutional theoretical perspective could have been employed. To remedy this and other limitations, the final chapter of this book offers an extensive list of directions for further scholarly research and discusses some of these additional lenses.

Bibliography

Ackroyd, S., & Karlsson, J. C. (2014). Critical realism, research techniques, and research designs. In P. K. Edwards, J. O'Mahoney, & S. Vincent (Eds.), *Studying organizations using critical realism: A practical guide* (pp. 21–45). Oxford University Press.

Bartlett, L., & Vavrus, F. (2017). Comparative case studies: An innovative approach. *Nordic Journal of Comparative and International Education, 1*(1), 5–17. https://doi.org/10.7577/njcie.1929.

Bhaskar, R. (1978). On the possibility of social scientific knowledge and the limits of naturalism. *Journal for the Theory of Social Behaviour, 8*(1), 1–28.

Bhaskar, R. (2014). Forward. In P. K. Edwards, J. O'Mahoney, & S. Vincent (Eds.), *Studying organizations using critical realism: A practical guide* (pp. v–xv). Oxford University Press.

Briner, R. B., & Denyer, D. (2012). Systematic review and evidence synthesis as a practice and scholarship too. In D. M. Rousseau (Ed.), *The Oxford handbook of evidence-based management* (pp. 112–129). Oxford University Press.

Callahan, J. L. (2010). Constructing a manuscript: Distinguishing integrative literature reviews and conceptual and theory articles. *Human Resource Development Review, 9*(3), 300–304.

Crocco, O. S., & Bunwirat, N. (2014). English in ASEAN: Key effects. *International Journal of the Computer, the Internet and Management, 22*(2), 22–27.

Crocco, O. S., Nguyen, L., & Tkachenko, O. (2021). Vietnam and regional human resource development in ASEAN. In H. T. Tran, T. T. Phuong, H. T. M. Van, & G. N. McLean (Eds.), *Human resource development in Vietnam: Research and practice* (pp. 97–117). Palgrave Macmillan. https://doi.org/10.1007/978-3-030-51533-1_4.

Crocco, O. S., & Tkachenko, O. (2020). Regional human resource development: The case of Southeast Asia and ASEAN. *Human Resource Development International*. https://doi.org/10.1080/13678868.2020.1858261.

Denyer, D., & Tranfield, D. (2009). Producing a systematic review. In D. A. Buchanan & A. Bryman (Eds.), *The SAGE handbook of organizational research methods* (pp. 671–689). SAGE.

Destradi, S. (2020). The finances of the Association of Southeast Asian Nations (ASEAN). In U. Engel & F. Mattheis (Eds.), *The finances of regional organizations in the Global South* (pp. 206–220). Routledge.

Edwards, P. K., O'Mahoney, J., & Vincent, J. (Eds.). (2014). *Studying organizations using critical realism: A practical guide*. Oxford University Press.

England, K. V. (1994). Getting personal: Reflexivity, positionality, and feminist research. *The Professional Geographer, 46*(1), 80–89.

Garavan, T., McCarthy, A., & Carbery, R. (2019). An ecosystems perspective on international human resource development: A meta-synthesis of the literature. *Human Resource Development Review, 18*(2), 248–288. https://doi.org/10.1177/1534484319828865.

Gentile, E. (Ed.). (2019). *Skilled labor mobility and migration: Challenges and opportunities for the ASEAN Economic Community*. Asian Development Bank and Edward Elgar Publishing.

Grimaldi, E., Serpieri, R., & Spano, E. (2015). Positionality, symbolic violence and reflexivity: Researching the educational strategies of marginalised groups.

In K. Bhopal & R. Deuchar (Eds.), *Researching marginalized groups* (pp. 134–148). Routledge.

Gough, D., Thomas, J., & Oliver, S. (2012). Clarifying differences between review designs and methods. *Systematic Reviews, 1*, Article 28.

Hsieh, H., & Shannon, S. E. (2005). Three approaches to qualitative content analysis. *Qualitative Health Research, 15*(9), 1277–1288.

Joffe, H., & Yardley, L. (2004). Content and thematic analysis. *Research methods for clinical and health psychology.*

Karr, J., Lokshin, B., & Loh, K. (2020). *The future of work across ASEAN: Policy prerequisites for the Fourth Industrial Revolution.* The Asia Foundation.

Mahbubani, K., & Sng, J. (2017). *The ASEAN miracle: A catalyst for peace.* Ridge Books.

Mingers, J. (2014). *Systems thinking, critical realism and philosophy: A confluence of ideas.* Routledge.

Rattanasevee, P. (2014). Towards institutionalised regionalism: The role of institutions and prospects for institutionalisation in ASEAN. *SpringerPlus, 3*(556), 1–10. http://www.springerplus.com/content/3/1/556.

Ryan, G. W., & Bernard, H. R. (2003). Techniques to identify themes. *Field Methods, 15*(1), 85–109.

Sandelowski, M., & Barroso, M. (2007). *Handbook for synthesizing qualitative research.* Springer.

Severino, R. C. (1999). ASEAN and the media: Shortcomings in regional press reporting "Where are the facts?" *Asian Media Report.* Available at https://asean.org/?static_post=asean-and-the-media-shortcomings-in-regional-press-reporting-where-are-the-facts-by-rodolfo-c-severino-secretary-general-of-asean-this-article-appeared-in-asian-media-report-january-1999-2.

Stagers, M. (2016). *Data quality in Southeast Asia: Analysis of official statistics and their institutional framework as a basis for capacity building and policy making in the ASEAN.* Palgrave Macmillan.

Torraco, R. J. (2005). Writing integrative literature reviews: Guidelines and examples. *Human Resource Development Review, 4*(3), 356–367.

Torraco, R. J. (2016). Writing integrative literature reviews: Using the past and present to explore the future. *Human Resource Development Review, 15*(4), 404–428. https://doi.org/10.1177/1534484316671606.

Tranfield, D., Denyer, D., & Smart, P. (2003). Toward a methodology for developing evidence-informed management knowledge by means of systematic review. *British Journal of Management, 14*, 207–222.

Vincent, S., & Wapshott, R. (2014). Critical realism and the organizational case study: A guide to discovering institutional mechanisms. In P. K. Edwards, J. O'Mahoney, & S. Vincent (Eds.), *Studying organizations using critical realism: A practical guide* (pp. 148–167). Oxford University Press.

PART II

The Human Resource Development Ecosystem of Southeast Asia

CHAPTER 3

Culture, Policy, and ASEAN: The Macro Dimension

While HRD practitioners in Southeast Asia are often rightly concerned with what is happening in their organizations, there is a larger macro dimension of the Regional HRD ecosystem made up of components that "support and regulate" HRD in the region (Garavan et al., 2019, p. 259). These components of the macro dimension of the Regional HRD ecosystem include government actors that set policy for the implementation of HRD and HRD-related activities as well as cultural or other informal institutions that play a major role in shaping and facilitating HRD processes. These components work in concert, mutually influencing and enforcing one another.

3.1 The Centrality of Culture

The first component of the macro dimension in need of discussion due to its pervasiveness and relevance to Regional HRD is culture. While all human beings have a shared human nature in addition to individual personalities, culture makes up the "collective programming of the mind that distinguishes the members of one group or category of people from others" (Hofstede et al., 2010, p. 6). This programming includes values that drive practices. One core component of culture is cultural beliefs, which are "the shared ideas and thoughts that govern interactions among

O. S. Crocco, *Developing Human Resources in Southeast Asia*, Palgrave Macmillan Asian Business Series,
https://doi.org/10.1007/978-3-030-79697-6_3

individuals and between them, their gods, and other groups" (Greif, 2006, p. 269). Cultural characteristics are dynamic, evolving over time, and are informed by history, politics, language, and ethnicity. They represent what Scott (2014) calls the "cultural-cognitive elements," which are comprised of "the shared conceptions that constitute the nature of social reality and create the frames through which meaning is made" (p. 67).

Culture as a phenomenon exists at a national level, which can be understood as the broad cultural concepts that apply to a country's citizens as a whole. Culture also exists at the organizational, ethnic, sub-regional, and even global levels (Marquardt & Engel, 1993). For example, in addition to the national level (Hofstede, 2002; Hofstede et al., 2010; Trompenaars & Hampden-Turner, 2012), cultural characteristics have been studied at the organizational or corporate level (Chow & Liu, 2009; Schein, 2017) and even the continental level, such as Asian collectivism (Li, 2007). However, virtually no literature has been written about the implications of culture for Regional HRD, including for regional organizations such as ASEAN.

One can see that in a region like Southeast Asia with a regional organization such as ASEAN, 11 different national cultures, hundreds of ethnic cultures, and thousands of organizational cultures, there is a complex overlapping of cultural characteristics (see Table 3.1). The diverse characteristics of the 10 member states of ASEAN and Timor-Leste shape the

Table 3.1 Cultural characteristics

Country	*Uncertainty avoidance (practices)*	*Power distance (practices)*	*Collectivism (practices)*	*Human orientation (practices)*	*Performance orientation (practices)*	*Gender egalitarianism (practices)*
Indonesia	4.17	5.18	4.54	4.69	4.41	3.26
Malaysia	4.78	5.17	4.61	4.87	4.34	3.51
Philippines	3.89	5.44	4.65	5.12	4.47	3.64
Singapore	5.31	4.99	4.90	3.49	4.90	3.70
Thailand	3.93	5.63	4.03	4.81	3.93	3.35
Average	4.41	5.28	4.55	4.59	4.41	3.49
Globe Project averages	4.17	5.14	4.24	4.09	4.10	3.38

Note No data available for Brunei, Cambodia, Lao PDR, Myanmar, Timor-Leste, or Vietnam; however, upcoming edition is likely to include more Southeast Asian countries
Source Globe Project (n.d.)

paradigms and practices of the people, organizations, and countries of Southeast Asia, which, in turn, shape HRD policies, practices, and beliefs. The cultural characteristics of the region and the ability of the region to find harmony are also important considering ASEAN's espoused values of unity and diversity. Cultural diversity is treasured in ASEAN and celebrated through a multitude of celebratory initiatives such as the ASEAN Musical Extravaganza (ASEAN, 2012a). The preservation of culture and the acknowledgment that cultural traditions should be preserved are espoused in organizations like ASEAN, although arguably more realized within the majority cultural groups in the region.

While there are many points of cultural divergence in ASEAN, there are also notable points of convergence in both cultural characteristics and cultural celebrations. Take for example the various water celebrations (Poh, 2008), which include the new year water festivals of Songkran (Thailand), Thingyan (Myanmar), Chaul Chnam Thmey (Cambodia), and Boun Pi Mai (Lao PDR). In Cambodia, the Bonn Om Touk water festival marks the end of the rainy season when the water in the river remarkably reverses direction, a natural phenomenon important for the fertilization of the surrounding areas (Poh, 2008). There are additional festivals such as the Sea-Offering Ceremonies (Indonesia), Runsay Ritual (Philippines), and the Thaipusam Festival (Malaysia and Singapore).

Culture is also an important consideration when considering organizations in the region, especially as they continue to become more interconnected. Take for example the multinational corporations (MNCs) with local subsidiaries in Southeast Asian countries. We know from duality theory that MNCs experience "conflicting pressures towards and away from" local practices of subsidiaries (Brewster et al., 2008, p. 320). And local cultures have different views toward MNC policies on topics like work-life balance, which is historically a western concept (de Cieri & Bardoel, 2009). Research shows that the national culture of a local subsidiary influences the human resource and management practices of the MNC in that firm (Inma, 2007; Swierczek & Onishi, 2003). In a study on age discrimination in MNC subsidiaries in Thailand, Inma (2007) found that local Thai firms still use age as a hiring criterion, revealing that national culture sometimes overrides the organizational culture of an MNC. Prioritizing the national culture may be the result of organizations seeking to be congruent with local practices and thus more competitive in local markets (Inma, 2007). Either way, national culture is an undeniable factor in human resource and management practices, even in multinational subsidiaries. A multi-case study of German companies with subsidiaries in Thailand, Singapore, and Indonesia showed that there was some ambiguity and differences in the extent to which subsidiaries could modify the multinational's rules to reflect national culture (Stehle & Erwee, 2007).

Similarly, consider the role that culture plays in mergers and acquisitions (M&As) in the region. In the last two decades, there has been an increase of M&As in Southeast Asia, a trend likely to continue (Tang & Metwalli, 2006). When an acquiring company merges with a target firm in another country, there is a compounding of both national and organizational cultures. Within Asian contexts, Tang and Metwalli (2006) point out that cultural differences are the "most frequently quoted reasons for failure in cross-border M&A" and highlight the necessity of developing "a strategy for cultural integration before the merger" (p. 156). Cultural characteristics are thus important to consider to the extent to which they influence HRD activities and processes. But it is also important for HRD practitioners to consider the role of culture when designing training and learning experiences to facilitate effective M&A activity.

To illustrate the role of culture in HRD at the individual level, consider the case of Singaporeans considering an international assignment. As a primarily collectivist culture where social and family relationships are often prioritized over one's individual interests, Singaporeans who are considering work abroad were strongly influenced by the perceived influence that international assignment would have on their family (Zhu et al., 2006). In her study of the cultural adjustment of Thai workers in Cambodia, Lao PDR, Myanmar, and Vietnam, Pruetipibultham (2019) found that many of them struggled to adjust to the new culture.

Intercultural competence, or the ability to work and live effectively in cross-cultural and multicultural environments, is a relevant and important part of HRD as a field of study (Rosenbusch, 2015) but has been less of a focus in Asian contexts (van der Poel, 2016). This lack of focus is partly explained by the cultural context of many Asian countries, which have existing cultural values geared toward harmony and pragmatism (van der Poel, 2016). However, harmony and pragmatism are values that focus on finding common ground and minimizing differences so as to achieve a common goal. Thus, in a paradoxical sense, the cultural values of harmony and pragmatism can render the role of culture less visible in the Southeast Asian context as it relates to HRD and HRM scholarship.

Language is another important facet of culture that influences Regional HRD. While the official language and lingua franca of ASEAN is English (Kirkpatrick, 2010), the process of selecting and using English as the operative language in the region has been fraught with difficulty (Crocco & Bunwirat, 2014). This decision has become a driver of government policy as well as policies in organizations and universities, having implications for Regional HRD. The agreement to use English as the working language of the region has offered avenues for talent mobility and cross-cultural communication. English language skills can even become a form of competitive advantage for workers, as in the case of Indonesian engineers (Araminta & Halimi, 2015), and can thus influence education policy and course offerings. More often, however, the use of English has been something that "unites the elite" (Warner & Rowley, 2007, p. 177) rather than broadly supports HRD. The implications for HRD on this issue are vast. Consider the fact that all training activities coordinated by ASEAN are conducted in English. This policy means that a brilliant Cambodian architect wishing to participate in ASEAN-sponsored training in Singapore will have to do so in English. While English-language education in Cambodia is increasing, the policy immediately disenfranchises the vast majority of people who do not have English language proficiency at the level required to benefit from training conducted in that language.

Scratching the surface of language's influence in Regional HRD also reveals the importance of ethnicity as a component of culture in Southeast Asia (Rowley & Bhopal, 2005). Malaysia is a prime example of its importance, with an ethnic makeup of Malays (~60%), Malaysian-Chinese (~30%), and Malaysian-Indian (~10%) (Smith, 2003). Indonesia's largest ethnic group, the Javanese, only makes up around 40% of the total population and has over 10 ethnic minority groups with over two million people the largest of which is the Sundanese with over 36 million (Turner, 2018). In East Timor, only 36% of the population belongs to the Tetum Prasa-speaking ethnic majority. The least ethnically diverse countries in Southeast Asia are Cambodia with over 96% being Khmer, Thailand with over 90% being Thai (defined as speaking Thai only), and Vietnam with over 85% being Kinh (Vi^ẹt) (Turner, 2018).

Ethnicity plays a role in Regional HRD, particularly in its ability to influence social and business networks (discussed in Chapter 4). For example, the Chinese minority in Malaysia and Singapore, which have the largest percentage of Chinese of any of the Southeast Asian countries, offers certain advantages and resources to those ethnic groups in their cross-country relationships (Rowley & Warner, 2007). There is also evidence that cultural characteristics derived primarily from outside the region, and/or over time through migration, influence Regional HRD. In many small- and medium-sized enterprises (SMEs) in Southeast Asia, Chinese business culture dominates management practices (Bjerke, 2000).

Take the case of Indonesia, which has over 200 ethnic groups, different religious traditions, and the legacy of Dutch and Japanese colonization. Linked closely with culture is the role that history plays in Southeast Asia, particularly as it relates to a long history of intraregional conflict (Warner & Rowley, 2007). The unique multi-ethnic cultural context along with its history has influenced leadership and management in Indonesia (Munandar, 2003). For example, it can be argued that "no specific management science or style has developed in Indonesia" and, as a result, Indonesian leaders have been influenced largely by U.S. business culture and thus tends to be more pragmatic (Munandar, 2003, p. 82). Despite the vast ethnic diversity in Southeast Asia, government prioritization of nationalism has often led to policies that segregate, isolate, and minimize ethnic diversity instead of enhance it (Turner, 2018).

Religion is another component of culture. As described in Chapter 1, Southeast Asia is incredibly diverse from a religious standpoint. This is important for Regional HRD because religion can be a mechanism through which HRD is facilitated. The most obvious case of this is through religious higher education such as Islamic higher education in Indonesia (Nugraha et al., 2016). Religion-based NGOs, organizations associated with official religions, individuals motivated by religious convictions shape development generally in Southeast Asia by serving as a "channel through which the tangible drivers of development (such as money, aid and food) can flow" as well as an "initiator of developmental processes, a source of advocacy and influence, and the glue that binds communities together during processes of development-related upheaval and change" (Woods, 2018, p. 254). In this sense, religion, like culture generally, has the potential to influence funding for HRD-related projects at the national or organizational levels, motivate individuals to participate in HRD, and shape how organizations make decisions about who should receive HRD programming and how it should be facilitated within the organization. Religiosity can also influence entrepreneurial intention as was found in Indonesian SMEs (Sulung et al., 2020).

Culture, broadly defined, is "an important factor for determining societal organizations [and] influencing institutional development" (Greif, 2006, p. 270). Linked closely with and influenced by culture, there are other "formal and informal institutions" that make up the macro ecosystem (Garavan et al., 2019, p. 260). Here, institutions are not referring to actual organizations or physical entities, but rather to the formal and informal processes of "development, codification, communication, and enforcement" (Pahl-Wostl, 2009, p. 356). On the one hand, formal institutions are connected to and regulated by government, which makes them often legally-binding and associated with enforcement mechanisms. On the other hand, informal institutions refer to societal and cultural norms, some of which are explicitly written or documented but the vast majority of which are implicit within the culture. As a result, they are not legally enforceable but rather societally enforced by social rewards and punishments (Pahl-Wostl, 2009).

In addition to the aforementioned cultural-cognitive elements of institutions, there are also normative institutions and regulative institutions (Scott, 2014). Normative institutions are informal "shared but not codified rules of good practice" (Pahl-Wostl, 2009, p. 357). An example of a shared norm of good practice in the region is the principle of informality (Acharya, 1998). These also include frameworks such as the ASEAN Way, which has been agreed upon in various seminal ASEAN documents. Whether the ASEAN Way is more normative or regulative is perhaps up for debate. While the founders of ASEAN did not have an initial conceptualization of what would become the ASEAN identity (Acharya, 2001), it emerged via processes of cooperation and a combination of these formal and informal institutions. For example, the regulatory power of ASEAN to initiate consequences on its members is a stark contrast between ASEAN and another regional organization such as the EU (Pero, 2019). That said, there is a debate that ASEAN is becoming more regulatory given the rise of regional standards and qualification frameworks discussed throughout this book (Jones & Hameiri, 2020).

In its totality, the role of culture on Regional HRD is complex and reaches through history and across all levels of society in Southeast Asia. Culture's impact on Regional HRD is mutually constituting. In the case of the regional organization, ASEAN, Acharya (2001) points out that "it was not so much that culture created norms, norms also created culture" (p. 86).

3.2 The Regional Organization of ASEAN

The second component of the macro ecosystem is the regional organization ASEAN itself. ASEAN and its sectoral bodies are part of the macro ecosystem informing Regional HRD in Southeast Asia. ASEAN intentionally creates a regional infrastructure that sets formal and informal guidelines and policies for HRD for the region. As mentioned in Chapter 1, there are many ways that ASEAN is similar to other regional organizations like the European Union, the Union of South American Nations, and the South African Development Community. It is primarily the ASEAN Way that differentiates ASEAN from its regional counterparts.

It cannot be overstated that the key actors of ASEAN are the nation-states themselves (Weatherbee, 2019), which is why ASEAN has sought security from within the region instead of from extra-regional foreign powers (Tarling, 2010). While the initial purpose of ASEAN centered around maintaining the sovereignty of the countries of the region as well as stopping intra-regional conflict, the founding Bangkok Declaration included an additional purpose of "provid[ing] assistance to each other in the form of training and research facilities in the educational, professional, technical and administrative fields" (ASEAN, 1967). From the inception of ASEAN, there has been an understanding of the role of HRD and HRD-related processes in achieving its vision. As ASEAN expanded to include economic and socio-cultural aspirations, HRD's role also grew.

In the late 1970s, the member countries of ASEAN began to see HRD as a key mechanism for the national development of countries within the region (Luhulima, 1992). The increased emphasis on developing the workforces of the individual countries spread to ASEAN, which began shifting its focus to Regional HRD. In the Treaty of Amity and Cooperation in Southeast Asia of 1976, the ASEAN member countries further committed to "achieve the closest cooperation on the widest scale and shall seek to provide assistance to one another in the form of training and research facilities in the social, cultural, technical, scientific and administrative fields" (ASEAN, 1976). The ASEAN Charter, signed in 2007, further highlighted the role of HRD and HRD-related activities, devoting one of its 15 purposes to "develop human resources through closer cooperation in education and lifelong learning, and in science and technology, for the empowerment of the peoples of ASEAN and for the strengthening of the ASEAN Community" (ASEAN, 2012b, p. 3). These seminal documents show the importance of HRD to ASEAN's identity and purpose in the region.

In 2010, ASEAN published the ASEAN Leaders' Statement on Human Resources and Skills Development for Economic Recovery and Sustainable Growth (ASEAN, 2012c). The statement focused on the HRD-related goals of "technical cooperation and capacity-building activities" as well as the skills development of ASEAN workers, including the development of "national and regional human resource development plans and programmes" (ASEAN, 2012c, p. 22). Then, in 2020 at the 36th ASEAN Summit ASEAN published the ASEAN Declaration on Human Resources Development for the Changing World of Work, which outlined 15 HRD-related actions ASEAN plans to undertake to support its regional workforce (ASEAN, 2020a). The declaration included the broad goal to cultivate a "lifelong learning culture in societies and raise awareness of youth, workers and employers on the importance of investing in skills development to adapt to the changing world of work, including education and training" (ASEAN, 2020a, p. 3). It also mentioned many other aspects of HRD, such as developing skills for people with disabilities, supporting National HRD (NHRD) policy development, fostering "re-skilling" and "upskilling" in businesses, and promoting technical and vocational education and training (TVET), which includes the establishment of the ASEAN TVET Council for regional TVET coordination (ASEAN, 2020a, p. 4).

ASEAN represents part of the macro dimension of the Regional HRD ecosystem as it coordinates organizations, member country national governments, and extra-regional partners to facilitate HRD in the region. Many of the specific ways ASEAN coordinates will be expounded upon in subsequent dimensions of the Regional HRD ecosystem, but it is important to keep in mind at the outset that ASEAN itself is an important overarching player in the ecosystem.

ASEAN facilitates HRD in the region through a host of mechanisms, an exhaustive list of which is not possible here. Perhaps most notable is the ASEAN Labour Ministers (ALM) Meeting, which is one of the ministerial bodies under the ASEAN Socio-Cultural Community. The ALM leads the ASEAN Skills Competition every two years, each of which centers around a different HRD area of relevance for the region. ALM also coordinates the ASEAN Human Resources Conference as a way of synthesizing learning around HRD in the region and sharing lessons learned with regional stakeholders. Other ASEAN sectoral bodies and stakeholders that play key roles in HRD policy and practice in the region include the Senior Labour Ministers Meeting (SLOM), the Senior Officials Meeting on Education (SOM-ED), the ASEAN TVET Council, and the ASEAN Future Workforce Council (AFWC). Then, there is a slew of related ASEAN sectoral bodies and stakeholders that work in conjunction with one another to bring about HRD and related policy and practice. These include, for example, the ASEAN Qualification Reference Framework (AQRF) discussed below, the ASEAN Business Advisory Council, which advises businesses and economic ministers of member countries about private sector priorities amidst economic integration, the ASEAN Coordinating Committee on Small and Medium Enterprises, which espouses HRD as one of its strategic goals in its 2016–2025 strategic plan (ASEAN, 2019a), the ASEAN Confederation of Employers (ACE), which is discussed in Chapter 4, and the aforementioned AUN.

There are also important Regional HRD approaches that are introduced by other stakeholders (e.g., individuals and organizations) in a variety of fields and topics. For example, Abdullah (2018) writes about training activities related to neurotechnology, a "bottom-up approach" that he envisions leading to something like the creation of the "ASEAN Brain, Mind, Behaviour and Neuroscience Institute for Creativity" (p. 1).

ASEAN itself is not a wealthy organization (each member contributes only what the poorest country can contribute), and the vast majority of the funds go to continuing the work of the ASEAN Secretariat located in Jakarta, which organizes and coordinates regional organization's efforts and serves as its headquarters. Its limited budget means that ASEAN largely plays the role of facilitator in the region, as evidenced by its facilitation of Regional HRD. It is the member countries of ASEAN, often in conjunction with extra-regional partners (e.g., Japan, China, Australia), that carry out both the activities of Regional HRD and the funding for those activities. Thus, most central to implementing the collective vision of ASEAN for Regional HRD in Southeast Asia is the role of the national governments of ASEAN's member states.

3.3 Government Support and Regulation

Government support and regulation of HRD within the 11 individual Southeast Asian countries makes up the third dimension of the macro ecosystem. Each country within Southeast Asia has policies and regulations that facilitate NHRD to varying degrees. Typically, these policies and regulations emerge from national strategic development plans such as Brunei Vision 2035 (Wawasan Brunei 2035), which aspires to have "highly skilled people measured by the highest international standards" (Government of Brunei Darussalam, n.d.). As a result, the quality and characteristics of education, skill development, and training differ widely throughout the region. Thus, an important reality of Regional HRD is that the diverse NHRD systems influence the character and processes of Regional HRD.

Individual countries and their political leadership play an important and ongoing role in regional community-building as well (Pero, 2019). In the ASEAN Leaders' Statement on Human Resources and Skills Development for Economic Recovery and Sustainable Growth (ASEAN, 2010), the role of governments is prioritized in the goal of fostering "national and regional social dialogue among government, employers and workers in addressing human resource development, policies and programmes" (ASEAN, 2010). As part of this statement, ASEAN recognized that Regional HRD is something interconnected with its member governments and organizations.

Why do governments play such a crucial role in Regional HRD? Most importantly, they set policies and provide funding for HRD to support skill development. Despite its importance, Abonyi and Slyke (2010) point out that recognizing the role of skill development and training remains one of the overarching governmental challenges facing Southeast Asian countries. In particular, skill development and training are needed for local suppliers, especially SMEs, who need basic technical skills and management skills to stay competitive in regional and global value chains (Abonyi & Slyke, 2010). While HRD is often considered the purview of individual organizations more than governments, it is understood in ASEAN member countries that both companies and governments are responsible for ensuring that the workforce is competent (ASEAN, 2001). Thus, skill development and training provide an important intersection between the private and public sectors. Companies provide a variety of HRD interventions such as on-the-job training, training programs, and mechanisms that facilitate HRD. Governments, on the other hand, provide policies and regulations for training institutions as well as incentives and other support for HRD (ASEAN, 2001). While the private sector is engaged in a variety of HRD-related tasks and initiatives, ASEAN has had "only fragmented positions" as they relate to the private sector (Severino, 2015, p. 20).

The role played by national governments in HRD in Southeast Asia can be viewed in a variety of contexts. To reach its over 17,000 islands, the Indonesian government in the 1970s worked with the World Bank to create and then expand a Distance Training Program, which involved the use of its domestic satellite system (Marquardt & Engel, 1993). Thailand's Department of Skill Development under the Ministry of Labour and Social Welfare (1996), which began in 1992, had already begun to recognize shortages in skilled labor and sought to counteract these shortages by promoting skill development through vocational training and a Skill Development Fund that would allow employers to apply for governmental loans to facilitate upskilling. Many other countries in Southeast Asia have comparable funds. Also, governments are typically largely responsible for funding and implementing HRD-related initiatives in TVET for their respective countries. In countries like Cambodia, while the TVET strategy is largely set by the government, nearly two-thirds of the organizations providing TVET are either private TVET institutes or NGOs (Yok et al., 2019).

In a report on the role of government in Southeast Asia, OECD/ADB (2019) describes government involvement in human resource management (HRM), e.g., employee performance assessment, remuneration, etc., in the region (minus Myanmar and Timor-Leste). In this report, OECD/ADB (2019) shows that HRM functions in the region are largely centralized. Take, for example, data on employee performance, which are collected and standardized centrally in Brunei, Malaysia, the Philippines, and Vietnam whereas Thailand and Singapore collect and hold this data in a standardized form at the ministry level. Cambodia, Indonesia, and Lao PDR collect this information through different ministries and agencies but not in a standardized form (OECD, 2019). By and large, however, Brunei and Malaysia are reported as having the least delegation of HRM decisions to ministries, departments, or agencies while the Philippines and Vietnam are reported as having the highest levels of overall delegation (OECD/ADB, 2019). The report also found that competency management, which has to do with qualification frameworks and skill development, is a "high priority" for six Southeast Asian countries: Indonesia, Lao PDR, Malaysia, the Philippines, Singapore, and Thailand.

While it is beyond the scope of this book to delve deeply into the 11 NHRD systems of Southeast Asia, Singapore provides a compelling illustration of the role of the government in promoting HRD. Since separating from Malaysia in 1965, the Singaporean government has been intimately involved in shaping HRD policy, which includes a model for development that has been largely "state-driven, foreign-led, [and] export-oriented" (Pang & Lim, 2015, p. 19). This model has come with costs, namely high levels of turnover as highly skilled foreign professionals often return to their home countries. With little natural resources, the government has invested heavily in education and training (Ismail & Rasdi, 2016), and the development of its human resources has been the "single most important strategic capital for Singapore" (Osman-Gani, 2004, p. 276). One example of this strategy has been the creation and promulgation of technical and vocational education and training, which complements traditional higher education in the country and is closely aligned with national economic priorities (Ismail & Rasdi, 2016).

The Singaporean government also enacted several important policies that promoted HRD in the country. These include, but are not limited to, the Skills Development Levy Act, which was introduced in 1979 but not fully enacted until 2008, that takes a small percentage of an employee's salary and puts it into a Skills Development Fund. The Skills Development Fund is then controlled by the Ministry of Manpower, which uses it to provide incentives to organizations offering skill development programs to employees (Ismail & Rasdi, 2016). Singapore is also a good example of a national government intervening in the social system "to promote values and attitudes favorable to nation-building, self-reliance and hard work" (Pang & Lim, 2015, p. 4). As Singapore demonstrates, HRD at the organizational level is inextricably connected to the macro dimension of government support and regulation.

While each government sets its own policy, regulations, and investments related to HRD (e.g., Thailand's Professional Qualification Institute, Indonesia's Baden Nasional Sertifikasi Profesi), ASEAN plays a role as well. For example, in an effort to align skill qualification frameworks in the region, ASEAN created the AQRF, which is a regional mechanism designed to support standardization and competency certification across a host of knowledge and skill areas (ASEAN, 2016a; Table 3.2). Each of the 10 member states of ASEAN has their own national qualification frameworks, although at various phases, and regulate education and training in different ways. The AQRF was inspired in part by the

Table 3.2 Key governmental bodies associated with HRD

Country	*Main competency governmental body*	*Website*
Brunei	Ministry of Education	http://moe.gov.bn/SitePages/Homepage.aspx
Cambodia	National Training Board	http://www.ntb.gov.kh/
Indonesia	Badan Nasional Sertifikasi Profesi Ministry of Manpower	www.bnsp.go.id https://www.kemnaker.go.id
Lao PDR	Department of Skills Development and Employment—Ministry of Labour and Social Welfare	www.molsw.gov.la/
Malaysia	Malaysian Qualifications Agency Department of Skills Development Malaysia	https://mqa.gov.my www.dsd.gov.my
Myanmar	National Skills Standards Authority	https://nssa.gov.mm/
Philippines	Technical Education and Skills Development Authority	http://www.tesda.gov.ph/
Singapore	Ministry of Education Ministry of Manpower	https://www.moe.gov.sg https://www.mom.gov.sg
Thailand	Department of Skill Development Thai Industrial Standards Institute	http://www.dsd.go.th https://www.tisi.go.th/
Timor-Leste	Ministry of Education and Culture	http://gov.east-timor.org
Vietnam	Skills Development Department, General Directorate of Vocational Training, Ministry of Labor, Invalids and Social Affairs	http://www.molisa.gov.vn/Pages/trangchu.aspx

ASEAN Charter's intent to create a mostly free flow of skilled labor in the region. Thus, national governments have been amenable to working toward aligning their qualification frameworks with the AQRF. Countries such as Indonesia, Malaysia, and Thailand have already aligned their national qualifications frameworks with the AQRF, and other countries are seeking to do so as well (Table 3.2).

Given the diversity of political systems within ASEAN member countries, such as communism, one would assume that they could potentially manipulate the means and ends of HRD. However, examples of alignment in understanding the purposes and meaning of HRD are found in other relationships, like the mutual recognition arrangements (discussed below) and the ASEAN Skills Competition. These examples reflect a greater alignment with what it means to be skilled and how those skills are used. Even more alignments between the diverse Southeast Asian countries are revealed when considering labor mobility.

3.4 Regional Talent Mobility

The last macro dimension of the Regional HRD ecosystem includes regional talent mobility. While labor migration out of the region in the form of a brain drain has been a policy issue in Southeast Asia for many years (Abella, 1984), much of the migration of Southeast Asian citizens occurs within the region. According to the United Nations World Migration Report 2020, 6.8 million of the total 10 million migrants in the region are from Southeast Asian countries (United Nations, 2019a). Intra-regional migration occurs for a variety of reasons such as income differentials, labor productivity, changes in workforce demographics, technological developments, and improvements in ease of transportation (Syzdykova et al., 2020). As global markets interact, workforce mobility occurs more readily.

To understand this phenomenon, it is worth exploring the nature of intra-Southeast Asian migration, the vast majority of which relates to workers. International labor migration, even within a regional context such as Southeast Asia, is a complex phenomenon due in part to the fact that migrant due in part to the fact that it is difficult to disaggregate which migrants can be considered strictly labor migrants and which are "forced migrants," i.e., asylum seekers, refugees, etc. (Lee, 2019, p. 136). There are other challenges with data availability and lack of clear data categorization that influence analysis of regional talent mobility in Southeast Asia (Raymer et al., 2019).

Intra-Southeast Asian migration from 1990 until 2019 when the most recent data was collected by the United Nations (2019b), shows that in 1990 no Southeast Asian countries had a majority of their migrants end up in Southeast Asian countries (see Table 3.3). The country with the highest percentage of intra-Southeast Asian migrants was Malaysia with 43% of its migrants residing in other Southeast Asian countries. However, in 2019, five of the 11 Southeast Asian countries have a majority of their migrants residing in other Southeast Asian countries. This means that Southeast Asian countries have become increasingly popular for fellow Southeast Asian citizens who migrate. Thailand tops the list in terms of attracting Southeast Asian migrants with nearly 3.5 million migrants in 2019, which is more than all the other 10 Southeast Asian countries combined. This includes migrants from every Southeast Asian country by Timor-Leste and includes a massive 1.8 million migrants from Myanmar, over 900,000 from Lao PDR, and over 600,000 from Cambodia, its most

Table 3.3 Intra-Southeast Asian migration (1990 and 2019)

Country	*1990 migrants to other Southeast Asian countries*	*1990 percent of total migrants*	*2019 migrants to other Southeast Asian countries*	*2019 percent of total migrants*
Brunei	3,340	13%	7,044	15%
Cambodia	104,579	29%	710,326	65%
Indonesia	287,178	18%	1,386,693	31%
Lao PDR	170,494	35%	942,780	70%
Malaysia	242,549	43%	1,009,190	60%
Myanmar	235,518	34%	2,219,871	60%
Philippines	119,154	6%	150,179	3%
Singapore	38,464	25%	119,830	35%
Thailand	58,578	19%	119,660	12%
Timor-Leste	736	7%	23,669	60%
Vietnam	80,715	7%	166,675	4%

Source United Nations (2019b)

economically disadvantaged neighbors (see Table 3.4). The least popular destinations in 2019 were Timor-Leste, Myanmar, and the Philippines.

Increases in intra-Southeast Asian migration can largely be attributed to the work of ASEAN in this area (Lee, 2019). In ASEAN, effective talent mobility within the region is seen as crucial to economic and cultural integration. The ASEAN Free Trade Area (ASEAN, 1992) began the process of establishing a regional commitment to intraregional talent mobility (Abella, 2006). Building on its success, the ASEAN Framework Agreement on Services (ASEAN, 1995) laid the groundwork for the mutual recognition of a skilled workforce within the region. ASEAN also sought to facilitate easier travel in the region through the ASEAN Framework Agreement on Visa Exception, which allows short trips of 14 days for citizens of ASEAN member states. Recently, most of the impetus for regional talent mobility in ASEAN member states has come from the ASEAN Economic Community (AEC), established in 2015, which espouses the mostly free flow of skilled labor within the region.

As a result, talent mobility is tied to HRD in the region. In 2012, ASEAN held its 3rd Human Resource Conference entitled "Skills Development towards a Greater Mobility of Skilled Labour in ASEAN" (ASEAN, 2012d). At this conference, the ASEAN member states agreed on the need to continue developing their national skill frameworks and working towards regional skill frameworks. This goal is pursued largely

Table 3.4 Intra-Southeast Asian migration origins and destinations

Origin	*Destination*										
	Brunei	*Cambodia*	*Indonesia*	*Lao PDR*	*Malaysia*	*Myanmar*	*Philippines*	*Singapore*	*Thailand*	*Timor-Leste*	*Vietnam*
Brunei	–	0	6,639	0	52,001	0	14,492	1,659	15,491	0	0
Cambodia	0	–	111	276	182	55	161	130	32,758	0	38,744
Indonesia	0	0	–	0	2,363	0	4,203	23,524	23,524	23,524	0
Lao PDR	0	3,634	0	–	0	3,005	0	0	3,490	0	20,076
Malaysia	6960	16,166	1,225,156	0	–	345,947	116,423	91,002	15,580	0	99,875
Myanmar	0	0		0	0	–	0	0	0	0	0
Philippines	84	40	3,407	296	817	434	–	845	350	145	425
Singapore	0	0	138,338	0	952,261	0	13,044	–	16,329	0	0
Thailand	0	689,451	699	934,936	1,369	1,858,735	1,366	760	–	0	7,350
Timor-Leste	0	0	4,126	0	64	0	372	80	61	–	205
Vietnam	0	1,035	8,217	7,272	133	11,695	118	1,830	12,077	0	–

Source United Nations (2019b)

through collaboration with "TVET institutions, industry and social partners" in the region (ASEAN, 2012d, p. 10). However, in 2014, on the eve of the establishment of the AEC, a sobering report by the International Labour Organization and Asian Development Bank (2014) identified major skills gaps in the region as a barrier to regional integration. As a result, ASEAN ramped up its investment in technical vocational education and training (TVET) to boost the region's talent, as described in the ASEAN Work Plan on Education 2016–2020. In the later Master Plan on ASEAN Connectivity 2025, people mobility is one of the five strategic objectives oriented toward reducing "gaps between vocational skills demand and supply across ASEAN" (ASEAN, 2016a, p. 7; Table 3.5). This reduction is largely achieved through training initiatives and policy harmonization centered around the aforementioned AQRF, but there are many other programs and policies with both intra- and extra-regional partners, such as the ASEAN-ROK TVET for ASEAN Mobility (TEAM) Project (ASEAN, 2020b) (Table 3.5).

Another key mechanism for facilitating regional talent mobility is mutual recognition arrangements (MRAs), which allow individuals in

Table 3.5 Talent mobility and economic factors

Country	*Labor productivity*	*Skilled labor (% of labor force)*	*Number of migrants received from other Southeast Asian countries (2019)*	*Percentage of all intra-Southeast Asian migrants (2019)*
Brunei	$159,118	78.8%	90,282	1.31%
Cambodia	$7250	14.3%	72,417	1.06%
Indonesia	$25,412	42.0%	77,138	1.13%
Lao PDR	$13,144	34.2%	30,205	0.44%
Malaysia	$61,291	66.8%	1,917,109	27.96%
Myanmar	$13,905	28.1%	0	0%
Philippines	$20,433	29.9%	6,843	0.10%
Singapore	$151,522	84%	1,119,972	16.34%
Thailand	$31,204	38.8%	3,494,666	50.97%
Timor-Leste	$17,284	28.3%	4,908	0.07%
Vietnam	$11,970	39.4%	42,377	0.62%

Note Labor Productivity as defined by output per worker in GDP constant 2011 international $ in PPP, 2019

Source International Labor Organization (n.d.), United Nations Development Program (2020) and United Nations (2019b)

certain professions to work throughout the region once their qualifications have been approved by ASEAN. Between 2005 and 2014, MRAs were developed for professional engineers, nurses, architects, tourism professionals, medical practitioners, dentists, accountants, and surveyors. Each MRA is overseen by one or more regional bodies/entities within ASEAN (Mendoza & Sugiyarto, 2017). For example, the medical practitioner MRA is overseen by the ASEAN Joint Coordinating Committee on Medical Practitioners (ASEAN, n.d.), and the architecture MRA is overseen by the ASEAN Architect Council (AAC) and the ASEAN Architect Register (AAC, n.d.) all of which meet several times throughout the year. This mechanism means that once certified under an ASEAN MRA, a worker does not have to pursue country-specific certification in each ASEAN member state. This type of agreement is especially compelling for countries like Singapore, which has long sought to attract labor through migration policies that make it easier for highly skilled workers to migrate and near impossible for unskilled workers (Pang, 1992).

While impressive on paper and touted as a great achievement in regional talent mobility, the potential of MRAs has yet to be realized. This delayed potential is partly due to the fact that in countries such as Lao PDR, only 1.3% of workers are employed in one of the professions covered by MRAs (Phoumilay, 2019). Furthermore, even after workers are certified to work in other ASEAN countries, many personal and professional issues influence their decision to leave, such as migration costs, psychological costs of leaving family and social networks, difficulties with language, wage differentials, and cultural differences (Paweenawat & Vechbanyongratana, 2019). These issues may explain why, in most ASEAN member states, less than 3% of highly skilled jobs are filled by migrants (Kikkawa & Suan, 2019). MRAs also serve the purpose of spurring on national governments, especially those in the lower-middle-income category, to develop their national qualification frameworks in a way that aligns with ASEAN's frameworks. There is evidence that this is what has occurred in the medical field in Cambodia (Law et al., 2019).While MRAs and attempts to align qualification frameworks support regional talent mobility, "effectively implementing the MRAs also requires a concerted effort toward capacity building at both the national and regional level" (Mendoza & Sugiyarto, 2017, p. x). Given these regional-level policies and mechanisms, the availability and mobility of regional talent functions differently from that of national or global talent.

Talent mobility affects individual countries in different ways. In the case of Thailand, the Thai government has sought to recruit high-skilled foreign workers as a way of breaking out of the so-called middle-income trap in its national strategic plan of 2018–2037 (Office of the National Economic and Social Development Board, 2018). Using econometric modeling, Tipayalai (2020) found that high-skilled immigrants to Thailand contributed positively to economic growth as well as the overall labor productivity.

In the case of Southeast Asia and ASEAN, talent mobility occurs over short- and long-term periods in one or multiple locations. For migrant workers and the organizations that hire them to be successful, there are a few important issues to highlight (ASEAN, 2017). First, the workforce mobility of migrants in the region is influenced primarily by national policy frameworks and governance mechanisms. Despite the creation of MRAs, there is no guiding ASEAN policy related strictly to talent mobility. Therefore, ASEAN member states do a variety of different things. For example, Brunei and Vietnam have more centrally directed systems for the education and safe migration of migrant workers, whereas Indonesia, Myanmar, the Philippines, and Thailand have a mix of public and private training providers. In the latter countries, the governments set standards and leave it up to businesses and NGOs to initiate actions that satisfy the standards. On the other side of the spectrum are Lao PDR, Cambodia, and Malaysia, which have more laissez-faire systems. This allows companies such as the import–export company Dao-Heung Group based in Lao PDR to be made up of around 70% Laotians and roughly 30% Thai and Vietnamese workers (Park et al., 2017).

Some countries require pre-departure programs while others leave it up to the recruiting agency. For example, Indonesia, the Philippines, Thailand, and Vietnam require pre-departure programs for all outgoing workers. Singapore does as well for a variety of occupations. Cambodia, Lao PDR, and Myanmar require the recruiting agency to be responsible for pre-departure programs, although they are known for not following up on whether this requirement has been met (ASEAN, 2017). While some countries have ways of tracking these programs, there is no coordinated ASEAN policy or database that documents pre-departure training. There is also a lack of performance monitoring of migrant workers' programs, which makes it difficult to estimate the impact of migrant labor. While countries requiring pre-departure training cover topics such as "employment contracts, the rights and responsibilities of migrant workers, gender awareness, health problems faced by migrants, ways of coping with different forms of harassment and discrimination, and access to complaint mechanisms, such as the country's embassy in the receiving country," there is often not enough time to cover other important topics such as finance, banking, and family services (ASEAN, 2017, pp. 158–159). These topics carry a whole array of implications for Regional HRD policy and practice in Southeast Asia (discussed in Chapter 7).

ASEAN has shown a commitment to protecting the rights of migrant workers in the region. Key policy shifts included the ASEAN Declaration on the Protection and Promotion of the Rights of Migrant Workers in 2007 (ASEAN, 2007), which outlines general principles as well as the commitments of the member states to outgoing and incoming migrants. In addition, the Compendium on Migrant Workers' Education and Safe Migration Programmes (ASEAN, 2017) includes country reports and updates, and the Consensus on the Protection and Promotion of the Rights of Migrant Workers (ASEAN, 2019b) establishes regional protection for migrant workers, both documented and undocumented. ASEAN has also expressed interest in addressing human trafficking of migrants first described in the Bangkok Declaration on Irregular Migration 1999, the 1997 Declaration on Transnational Crime, and the 2004 Declaration Against Trafficking in Persons Particularly Women and Children, each of which recognizes the need to protect vulnerable populations and the need for additional protections (Lee, 2019).

While ASEAN is strategically placed to be a supportive actor in intraregional labor migration, its efforts are not free from scrutiny. When up against the ASEAN Way and the principle of non-interference in the internal affairs of member countries, ASEAN's efforts to ensure the protection of human rights are often stunted. This result is partly due to ASEAN's disconnectedness with civil society and the collective needs of the region's citizens (Allison-Reumann, 2017). Similarly, while many Southeast Asian countries have strong labor laws in place to support the rights of workers, enforcement has been weak (Manning & Pang, 1990). Labor movement in Southeast Asia is a sensitive topic, and while there are strategies in place for the movement of skilled labor, there is still no agreement on the migration of unskilled labor. Although labor migration has grown, options for migrant laborers to obtain citizenship in their new countries are often not available, which causes other complications for workers (Asis & Battistella, 2013).

Kelly (2018) has pointed out that migration outside the region has also been a source of human capital development; however, fewer of the people who migrate outside the region return to their Southeast Asian country of origin. Migrants' prospects for living and working outside the region are exemplified in the case of the Philippines, in which 10% of the population lives abroad and remittances account for 13% of the country's GDP (Phan & Coxhead, 2015). In the case of the rural Tagalog village in the Philippines, many migrants use their remittances to build houses in their home village of Tagalog as a means of providing for relatives and retaining a sense of connection (Aguilar, 2009). The rights of overseas workers and, in some cases such as that of the Philippines, the protection of these rights are of concern to churches, families, and NGOs in partnership with labor unions (Alcid, 2006). In a study of Indonesian female migrant workers, Aminuddin et al. (2019) found that the parents left behind in Indonesia faced a variety of economic and social consequences depending largely on whether the migrant daughter was married or not. Single workers were able to acquire more savings and send home remittances (Aminuddin et al., 2019). By and large, however, migration out of the region leads to a "skill drain" that likely cannot be compensated for by remittances (Ullah, 2018, p. 205).

The macro dimension of culture, a regional organization, government support and regulation, and regional talent mobility add to the dynamic and compelling nature of Southeast Asia as a region. In addition, these components highlight the complex environment in which human resources are developed in Southeast Asia. The macro dimension of Regional HRD discussed here, and other components functioning in a macro sense in this region, are worth exploring in more depth or even through other frameworks. The main point, however, is that when scholars and practitioners consider HRD activities and processes, doing so at the individual or organizational level alone will always be limited if the macro dimension is not also considered. They are powerful forces that shape the Regional HRD ecosystem. More direct influences on Regional HRD in Southeast Asia—the meso dimension of educational institutions, professional networks, international organizations and consultants, and family/peer networks—are explored in the next chapter.

3.5 The Components of the Macro Dimension in Concert: The Case of Vietnam

The relationship between a country's NHRD strategy and the Regional HRD ecosystem can be explored in the case of Vietnam. Vietnam joined ASEAN in 1995, which was around the same time as Lao PDR and Myanmar in 1997 and Cambodia in 1999. These countries (also called the CLMV countries as mentioned in Chapter 1) represent a development gap among ASEAN member states. Parenthetically, it is worth noting that if Timor-Leste was a full member of ASEAN, it would no doubt be included in this list, and, in recent years, Vietnam is often not included anymore in this categorization given its development gains.

The CLMV countries have been a focal point of Regional HRD efforts in an attempt to elevate the region's collective workforce and meet its economic integration goals. The case of Vietnam itself is instructive to see how government, ASEAN, and culture influence the Regional HRD ecosystem, which was explored in part by Crocco et al. (2021). Despite being a Communist state, the Communist Party of Vietnam reformed its economic system to be more market-oriented in 1986. Then, after joining ASEAN and seeing all the benefits that regional integration had to offer, the Vietnamese turned its sights toward HRD (Curry, 1996). Here we can see that not only does government regulation influence policy and implementation of HRD, but vast changes in government structure, as was seen in Vietnam, can have a cascading effect on HRD.

ASEAN has overseen three work plans related to the Initiative of ASEAN Integration (IAI), which have sought to bring all ASEAN member states on equal economic footing by elevating and investing in the CLMV countries. One of the core areas of the IAI has been HRD (ASEAN, 2016b). In fact, one of the five qualification criteria for IAI projects is that they contribute to "capacity building and human resource development" (ASEAN, 2016b, p. 49). As a result of the IAI, many projects related to HRD have been implemented to support Vietnam and the other CLMV countries. These include training courses and leadership development programs in a variety of areas such as communication, information technology, international relations, and construction (Crocco & Tkachenko, 2020).

Vietnam has not only been a beneficiary of ASEAN policies and practices related to HRD, but it has also had a firm hand in influencing Regional HRD priorities (Crocco et al., 2021). This can be seen most clearly in Vietnam's priorities during its last two stints as ASEAN Chair in 2010 and 2020. During these two periods of service as ASEAN Chair, significant gains have been made in ASEAN policy related to HRD, first in the aforementioned ASEAN Leaders' Statement on Human Resources and Skills Development for Economic Recovery and Sustainable Growth (ASEAN, 2012c) and then in the ASEAN Declaration on Human Resources Development for the Changing World of Work (ASEAN, 2020a). This is a clear example of the fact that in the Regional HRD ecosystem, the relationships between actors, even large actors like national governments and ASEAN itself, are not unidirectional. ASEAN influences the Regional HRD ecosystem by implementing HRD mechanisms, but the individual member countries also influence the priorities of ASEAN, in particular when they serve as chair.

The story of HRD in Vietnam also reveals that the unique cultural positionality of Vietnam influenced its conceptualization and implementation of HRD. In an analysis of Vietnam's historical and cultural influences on HRD, Truong et al. (2021) show that the indigenous cultural values and Confucianism have influenced HRD policy and practice in Vietnam. For example, as a result of its cultural values, education and training are highly valued in Vietnamese society and individuals often seek out opportunities to build on their knowledge and skills (Truong et al., 2021). However, given the social hierarchy and respect for superiors, this also means that many employees "have a reluctance to demonstrate creativity or take risks due to a fear of failure even after they have acquired new knowledge" (Truong et al., 2021, p. 18). Given the embeddedness of the Regional HRD ecosystem with the rest of the world, it is also important to note that global economic forces, political changes, and extra-regional forces influence Vietnam's stance toward HRD and the policies and practices that have emerged in the country.

Bibliography

Abdullah J. M. (2018). Hominem sine opus spatium: Where do the ideas come from to move the brain, mind, behaviour and neurosciences in Malaysia? *Malaysian Journal of Medical Sciences, 25*(2), 1–14. https://doi.org/10.21315/mjms2018.25.2.1.

Abella, M. I. (1984). Labour migration from South and South-East Asia: Some policy issues. *International Labour Review, 123*(4), 491–506.

Abella, M. (2006). Global competition for skilled workers and consequences. In C. Kuptsch & E. F. Pang (Eds.), *Competing for global talent* (pp. 11–32). International Institute for Labour Studies.

Abonyi, G., & Van Slyke, D. M. (2010). Governing on the edges. Globalization of production and the challenges to public administration in the twenty-first century. *Public Administration Review, 70*(Suppl), 33–45.

Acharya, A. (1998). Culture, security, multilateralism: The 'ASEAN way' and regional order. *Contemporary Security Policy, 19*(1), 55–84.

Acharya, A. (2001). *Constructing a security community in Southeast Asia: ASEAN and the problem of regional order.* Routledge.

Aguilar, F. (2009). Labour migration and ties of relatedness: Diaspora houses and investments in memory ion a rural Philippine village. *Thesis Eleven, 98*(1), 88–114.

Alcid, M. L. L. (2006). NGO-labor union cooperation in the promotion of the rights and interests of land based overseas Filipino workers. *Asian and Pacific Migration Journal, 15*(3), 335–357. https://doi.org/10.1177/011719680601500303.

Allison, L. (2015). *The EU, ASEAN and interregionalism: Regionalism support and norm diffusion between the EU and ASEAN.* Palgrave Macmillan.

Allison-Reumann, L. (2017). Integrating ASEAN in labor migration policy: From disjointed to complementary actor. *Asian Politics and Policy, 9*(3), 427–441. https://doi.org/10.1111/aspp.12329.

Aminuddin, M. F., Pallikadavath, S., Kamanda, A., Sukesi, K., Rosalinda, H., & Hatton, K. (2019). The social and economic impact of international female migration on left-behind parents in East Java, Indonesia. *Asian and Pacific Migration Journal, 28*(1), 97–114. https://doi.org/10.1177/0117196818815512.

Araminta, L. D. W., & Halimi, S. S. (2015). ASEAN economic community 2015: Needs analysis of Universitas Indonesia's engineering students. *Indonesian Journal of Applied Linguistics, 5*(1), 10–17. https://doi.org/10.17509/ijal.v5i1.841..

ASEAN Architect Council. (n.d.). *ASEAN mutual recognition arrangement on architectural services.* http://aseanarchitectcouncil.net/about-aac.

Association of Southeast Asian Nations. (n.d.). *Medical practitioners (AJCCM).* https://asean.org/asean-economic-community/sectoral-bodies-under-the-purview-of-aem/services/healthcare-services/medical-practitioners-ajccm/.

Association of Southeast Asian Nations. (1967). *The Bangkok Declaration.* ASEAN Secretariat. www.asean.org.

Association of Southeast Asian Nations. (1976). *Treaty of amity and cooperation in Southeast Asia.* ASEAN Secretariat. www.asean.org.

Association of Southeast Asian Nations. (1992). *Singapore Declaration of 1992*. https://asean.org/?static_post=singapore-declaration-of-1992-singapore-28-january-1992.

Association of Southeast Asian Nations. (1995, December 15). *ASEAN Framework Agreement on Services*. https://asean.org/?static_post=asean-framework-agreement-on-services.

Association of Southeast Asian Nations. (2001). *Preparing workers for changes in the labour market: The ASEAN Experience*. The ASEAN Secretariat.

Association of Southeast Asian Nations. (2007). *ASEAN declaration on the protection and promotion of the rights of migrant workers*. https://asean.org/?static_post=asean-declaration-on-the-protection-and-promotion-of-the-rights-of-migrant-workers.

Association of Southeast Asian Nations. (2010). *ASEAN leader's statement on human resources and skills development for economic recovery and sustainable growth*. https://asean.org/?static_post=asean-leaders-statement-on-human-resources-and-skills-development-for-economic-recovery-and-sustainable-growth.

Association of Southeast Asian Nations. (2012a). *Celebrate the rich and diverse cultures of ASEAN in "ASEAN musical extravaganza."* https://asean.org/celebrate-the-rich-and-diverse-cultures-of-asean-in-asean-musical-extravaganza/.

Association of Southeast Asian Nations. (2012b). *The ASEAN charter* (2nd ed.). The ASEAN Secretariat.

Association of Southeast Asian Nations. (2012c). *ASEAN Document Series 2010*. The ASEAN Secretariat.

Association of Southeast Asian Nations. (2012d). *Work plans of the subsidiary bodies of the ASEAN Senior Labour Officials Meeting (SLOM)*. The ASEAN Secretariat.

Association of Southeast Asian Nations. (2016a). *ASEAN guiding principles for quality assurance and recognition of competency certification systems*. The ASEAN Secretariat.

Association of Southeast Asian Nations. (2016b). *Initiative for ASEAN integration (IAI) work plan III*. https://asean.org/storage/2016/09/09rev2Content-IAI-Work-Plan-III.pdf.

Association of Southeast Asian Nations. (2017). *Compendium on migrant workers' education and safe migration programmes*. The ASEAN Secretariat.

Association of Southeast Asian Nations. (2019a). *ASEAN strategic action plan for SME development 2016–2025*. https://asean.org/storage/2012/05/3-SAP-SMED-Final.pdf.

Association of Southeast Asian Nations. (2019b). *ASEAN consensus on the protection and promotion of the rights of migrant workers*. https://asean.org/storage/2019/01/3.-March-2018-ASEAN-Consensus-on-the-Protection-and-Promotion-of-the-Rights-of-Migrant-Workers.pdf.

Association of Southeast Asian Nations. (2020a). *ASEAN declaration on human resources development for the changing world of work*. The ASEAN Secretariat. https://asean.org/storage/2020/06/ASEAN-Declaration-on-Human-Resources-Development-for-the-Changing-World-of-Work.pdf.

Association of Southeast Asian Nations. (2020b, October 1). *ASEAN, ROK launch ASEAN Mobility training project*. https://asean.org/asean-rok-launch-asean-mobility-training-project/

Asis, M. M. B., & Battistella, G. (2013). Multicultural realities and membership: States, migrations and citizenship in Asia. In L. A. Eng, F. L. Collins, & B. S. A. Yeah (Eds.), *Migration and diversity in Asian contexts* (pp. 31–55). ISEAS Publishing.

Bjerke, B. V. (2000). A typified, culture-based, interpretation of management of SMEs in Southeast Asia. *Asia Pacific Journal of Management, 17*(1), 103–132.

Brewster, C., Wood, G., & Brookes, M. (2008). Similarity, isomorphism or duality? Recent survey evidence on the human resource management policies of multinational corporations. *British Journal of Management, 19*, 320–342.

Chow, I. H. S., & Liu, S. S. (2009). The effect of aligning organizational culture and business strategy with HR systems on firm performance in Chinese enterprises. *The International Journal of Human Resource Management, 20*(11), 2292–2310.

Crocco, O. S., & Bunwirat, N. (2014). English in ASEAN: Key effects. *International Journal of the Computer, the Internet and Management, 22*(2), 22–27.

Crocco, O. S., Nguyen, L., & Tkachenko, O. (2021). Vietnam and regional human resource development in ASEAN. In H. T. Tran, T. T. Phuong, H. T. M. Van, & G. N. McLean (Eds.), *Human resource development in Vietnam: Research and practice* (pp. 97–117). Palgrave Macmillan. https://doi.org/10.1007/978-3-030-51533-1_4.

Crocco, O. S., & Tkachenko, O. (2020). Regional human resource development: The case of Southeast Asia and ASEAN. *Human Resource Development International*. https://doi.org/10.1080/13678868.2020.1858261.

Curry, R. L. (1996). Economic growth and transformation: Vietnam's challenge of human resource development. *ASEAN Economic Bulletin, 13*(2), 229–240.

De Cieri, H., & Bardoel, E. A. (2009). What does 'work-life management' mean in China and Southeast Asia for MNCs? *Community, Work & Family, 12*(2), 179–196. https://doi.org/10.1080/13668800902778959.

Garavan, T., McCarthy, A., & Carbery, R. (2019). An ecosystems perspective on international human resource development: A meta-synthesis of the literature. *Human Resource Development Review, 18*(2), 248–288. https://doi.org/10.1177/1534484319828865.

Garavan, T., McCarthy, A., & Morley, M. (2016). Global human resource development: Landscaping the anatomy of an evolving field. In T. Garavan, A. McCarthy, & M. Morley (Eds.), *Global human resource development: Regional and country perspectives* (pp. 1–16). Routledge.

Globe Project. (n.d.). An overview of the 2004 study: Understanding the relationship between national culture, societal effectiveness and desirable leadership attributes. https://globeproject.com/study_2004_2007?page_id=data#data.

Government of Brunei Darussalam. (n.d.). Wawasan Brunei 2035. https://www.gov.bn/SitePages/Wawasan%20Brunei%202035.aspx.

Greif, A. (2006). *Institutions and the path to the modern economy: Lessons from medieval trade*. Cambridge University Press.

Hofstede, G. (2002). *Culture's consequences: Comparing values, behaviors, institutions and organizations across nations*. Sage.

Hofstede, G., Hofstede, G.J., & Minkov, M. (2010). *Cultures and organizations: Software of the mind* (3rd ed.). McGraw-Hill.

Inma, C. (2007). Overt age discrimination in employment in Thailand: The ethical role of multinational corporations in human resource practices. In D. R. Sharpe & H. Hasegawa (Eds.), *New horizons in Asian management* (pp. 201–219). Palgrave Macmillan.

International Labour Organization. (n.d.). ILS Statistics. https://ilostat.ilo.org.

International Labour Organization and Asian Development Bank. (2014). *ASEAN Community 2015: Managing integration for better jobs and shared prosperity*. http://ilo.org/wcmsp5/groups/public/---asia/---ro-bangkok/documents/publication/wcms_300672.pdf.

Ismail, M., & Rasdi, R. M. (2016). Human resource development in Malaysia and Singapore. In T. N. Garavan, A. M. McCarthy, & M. J. Morley (Eds.), *Global human resource development: Regional and country perspectives* (pp. 104–127). Routledge.

Jones, L., & Hameiri, S. (2020). Southeast Asian regional governance: Political economy, regulatory regionalism and ASEAN integration. In T. Carroll, S. Hameiri, & L. Jones (Eds.), *The political economy of Southeast Asia: Politics and uneven development under hyperglobalisation* (4th ed., pp. 199–224). Palgrave Macmillan.

Kelly, P. (2018). Migration, development and remittances. In A. McGregor, L. Law, & F. Miller (Eds.), *Routledge handbook of Southeast Asian development* (pp. 198–210). Routledge.

Kikkawa, A., & Suan, E. B. (2019). Trends and patterns in intra-ASEAN migration. In E. Gentile (Ed.), *Skilled labor mobility and migration: Challenges and opportunities for the ASEAN Economic Community* (pp. 1–24). Edward Elgar Publishing.

Kirkpatrick, A. (2010). *English as a lingua franca in ASEAN: A multilingual model.* Hong Kong University Press.

Krapohl, S. (Ed.). (2017). *Regional integration in the global south.* Palgrave Macmillan.

Kuptsch, C., & Pang, E. F. (Eds.) (2006). *Competing for global talent.* International Institute for Labour Studies.

Law, K. M., Te, V., & Hill, P. S. (2019). Cambodia's health professionals and ASEAN mutual recognition arrangements: Registration, education and mobility. *Human Resources for Health, 17*, article no. 14, 1–9. https://doi.org/10.1186/s12960-019-0349-5.

Lee, C. (2019). Representing migration in ASEAN: Challenges to regional integration. In A. Idris & N. Kamaruddin (Eds.), *ASEAN post-50: Emerging issues and challenges* (pp. 135–154). Palgrave Macmillan.

Li, F. (2007). Asian collectivism and ethical decision-making. In D. R. Sharpe & H. Hasegawa (Eds.), *New horizons in Asian management* (pp. 40–54). Palgrave Macmillan.

Luhulima, C. P. F. (1992). Development co-operation in human resources: The ASEAN experience. In K. S. Sandhu, S. Siddique, C. Jeshurun, A. Rajah, J. L. H. Tan, & P. Thambipillai (Eds.), *The ASEAN reader* (pp. 281–285). Institute of Southeast Asian Studies.

Marquardt, M., & Engel, D. (1993). *Global human resource development.* Prentice Hall.

Manning, C., & Pang, E. F. (1990). Labour market trends and structures in ASEAN and the East Asian NIEs. *Asian-Pacific Economic Literature, 4*(2), 59–81.

Mendoza, D. R., & Sugiyarto, G. (2017). *The long road ahead: Status report on the implementation of the ASEAN mutual recognition arrangements on professional services.* Asian Development Bank.

Ministry of Labour and Social Welfare. (1996). *Department of skill development.* The Department of Skill Development, Thailand.

Munandar, A. S. (2003). Culture and management in Indonesia. In M. Warner (Ed.), *Culture and management in Asia* (pp. 82–98). Routledge.

Nugraha, M. S., Sahroni, D., & Latifah, A. (2016). Private Islamic higher education in ASEAN economic community (AEC) era. *Jurnal Pendidikan Islam, 2*(3), 393–412. https://doi.org/10.15575/jpi.v2i3.853.

Organisation for Economic Co-operation and Development/Asian Development Bank. (2019). *Government at glance Southeast Asia 2019.* OECD Publishing. https://doi.org/10.1787/9789264305915-en.

Office of the National Economic and Social Development Board. (2018). *National Strategy: 2018–2037 (Summary).* https://www.bic.moe.go.th/images/stories/pdf/National_Strategy_Summary.pdf.

Osman-Gani, A. M. (2004). Human capital development in Singapore: An analysis of national policy perspectives. *Advances in Developing Human Resources, 6*(3), 276–287. https://doi.org/10.1177/1523422304266074.

Pahl-Wostl, C. (2009). A conceptual framework for analyzing adaptive capacity and multi-level learning processes in resource governance regimes. *Global Environmental Change, 19*, 345–365.

Pang, E. F. (1992). Absorbing temporary foreign workers: The experience of Singapore. *Asian and Pacific Migration Journal, 1*(3–4), 495–509.

Pang, E. F., & Lim, L. Y. (2015). Labor, productivity and Singapore's development model. *The Singapore Economic Review, 60*(3), 1–30. https://doi.org/10.1142/S0217590815500332.

Park, S. H., Ungson, G. R., & Francisco, J. P. S. (2017). *ASEAN champions: Emerging stalwarts in regional integration*. Cambridge University Press.

Paweenawat, S. W., & Vechbanyongratana, J. (2019). Will ASEAN mutual recognition arrangements induce skilled workers to move? A case study of the engineering labor market in Thailand. In E. Gentile (Ed.), *Skilled labor mobility and migration: Challenges and opportunities for the ASEAN Economic Community* (pp. 241–266). Edward Elgar Publishing.

Pero, S. D. M. (2019). *Leadership in regional community-building: Comparing ASEAN and the European Union*. Palgrave Macmillan.

Peters, B. G. (2019). *Institutional theory in political science: The new institutionalism* (4th ed.). Edward Elgar Publishing.

Phan, D., & Coxhead, I. (2015). Education in Southeast Asia: Investments, achievements, and returns. In I. Coxhead (Ed.), *Routledge handbook of Southeast Asian economics* (pp. 249–269). Routledge.

Phoumilay, P. (2019). Vocational education and training in Lao PDR. In B. Bai & Paryono (Eds.), *Vocational education and training in ASEAN member states* (pp. 81–108). Springer.

Poh, L. (2008). *Celebrating the source: Water festivities of Southeast Asia*. The ASEAN Secretariat.

Pruetipibultham, Oranuch. (2019). *Cultural adjustment for working and living in the Mekong Sub-region countries (Cambodia, Lao PDR, Myanmar, Vietnam)* [การปรับตัวในวัฒนธรรมลุ่มน้ำโขง CLMV (กัมพูชา สปป.ลาวเมียนมาร์และเวียดนาม)] (in Thai). National Institute of Development Administration Publishing.

Raymer, J., Guan, Q., & Ha, J. T. (2019). Overcoming data limitations to obtain migration flows for ASEAN countries. *Asian and Pacific Migration Journal, 28*(4), 385–414. https://doi.org/10.1177/0117196819892344.

Rosenbusch, K. (2015). Intercultural competence and HRD. In R. F. Poell, T. S. Rocco, & G. L. Roth (Eds.), *The Routledge companion to human resource development* (pp. 592–605). Routledge.

Rowley, C., & Bhopal, M. (2005). The role of ethnicity in employment relations. *Asia Pacific Journal of Human Resources, 43*(3).

Rowley, C., & Warner, M. (2007). Introduction: Business and management in South East Asia. In C. Rowley & M. Warner (Eds.), *Management in South-East Asia* (pp. 1–13). Routledge.

Schein, E. H. (2017). *Organizational culture and leadership* (5th ed.). Wiley.

Scott, W. R. (2014). *Institutions and organizations: Ideas, interests, and identities* (4th ed.). Sage.

Severino, R. C. (2015). From political/security concerns to regional economic integration. In O. K. Beng, S. Basu Das, T. Chong, M. Cook, C. Lee., & M. Yeo (Eds.), *The 3rd ASEAN reader* (pp. 17–22). ISEAS Publishing.

Smith, W. A. (2003). Culture and management in Malaysia. In M. Warner (Ed.), *Culture and management in Asia* (pp. 115–134). Routledge.

Stehle, W., & Erwee, R. (2007). Transfer of human resource practices from German multinational enterprises to Asian subsidiaries. *Research and Practice in Human Resource Management, 15*(1), 63–88.

Sulung, L. A. K., Putri, N. I. S., Robbani, M. M., & Ririh, K. R. (2020). Religion, attitude, and entrepreneurial intention in Indonesia. *The South East Asian Journal of Management, 14*(1), 44–62. https://doi.org/10.21002/seam.v14i1.10898.

Swierczek, F. W., & Onishi, J. (2003). Culture and conflict: Japanese managers and Thai subordinates. *Personnel Review, 32*(1/2), 187–210. https://doi.org/10.1016/0148-2963(94)00003-W.

Syzdykova, Z., Medvedev, N., Suleymanova, S., Nazarova, E., & Volokh, V. (2020). Governance of cross-border migration in Asia. *Space and Culture, India, 7*(4), 264–273. https://doi.org/10.20896/saci.v7i4.568.

Tang, R. T. W., & Metwalli, A. M. (2006). *Mergers and Acquisitions in Asia: A global perspective*. Routledge.

Tarling, N. (2010). *Southeast Asia and the great powers*. Routledge.

Tipayalai, K. (2020). Impact of international labor migration on regional economic growth in Thailand. *Economic Structures, 9*(15), 1–19. https://doi.org/10.1186/s40008-020-00192-7.

Trompenaars, F., & Hampden-Turner, C. (2012). *Riding the waves of culture: Understanding diversity in global business* (2nd ed.). McGraw-Hill.

Truong, H. T. M., Pham, T. T. H., & Doan, T. T. T. (2021). Historical and cultural contexts of Vietnam affecting human resource development. In H. T. Tran, T. T. Phuong, H. T. M. Van, & G. N. McLean (Eds.), *Human resource development in Vietnam: Research and practice* (pp. 3–30). Palgrave Macmillan.

Turner, S. (2018). Ethnic minorities, indigenous groups and development tensions. In A. McGregor, L. Law, & F. Miller (Eds.), *Routledge handbook of Southeast Asian development* (pp. 224–237). Routledge.

Ullah, A. A. (2018). Skill drain from ASEAN countries: Can sending countries afford? *International Journal of Development Issues, 17*(2), 205–219. https://doi.org/10.1108/IJDI-12-2017-0210.

United Nations. (2019a). *World migration report 2020.* International Organization for Migration. https://www.un.org/sites/un2.un.org/files/wmr_2020.pdf.

United Nations. (2019b). *International Migrant Stock 2019.* https://www.un.org/en/development/desa/population/migration/data/estimates2/estimates19.asp.

United Nations Development Programme. (2020). *Human Development Reports.* http://hdr.undp.org/en.

Van der Poel, M. H. (2016). Asian human resource management and intercultural competence. In R. T. Segers (Ed.), *Multinational management: A casebook on Asia's global market leaders* (pp. 301–310). Springer.

Warner, M., & Rowley, C. (2007). Conclusion: Wither business and management in South East Asia? In C. Rowley & M. Warner (Eds.), *Management in South-East Asia* (pp. 175–181). Routledge.

Weatherbee, D. E. (2019). *ASEAN's half century: A political history of the Association of Southeast Asian Nations.* Rowman & Littlefield.

Woods, O. (2018). Religion and development in Southeast Asia. In A. McGregor, L. Law, & F. Miller (Eds.), *Routledge handbook of Southeast Asian development* (pp. 250–260). Routledge.

Yeates, N. (2019). World regional social governance, policy and development. In J. Midgley, R. Surender, & L. Alfers (Eds.), *Handbook of social policy and development* (pp. 224–245). Edward Elgar.

Yok, S., Chrea, S., & Pak, R. (2019). Technical and vocational education in training in Cambodia: Current status and future development. In B. Bai & Paryono (Eds.), *Vocational education and training in ASEAN member states: Current status and future development* (pp. 25–43). Springer.

Zhu, W., Luthans, F., Chew, I. K. H., & Li, C. (2006). Potential expats in Singaporean organizations. *Journal of Management Development, 25*(8), 763–776. https://doi.org/10.1108/02621710610684240.

CHAPTER 4

Education and Networks: The Meso Dimension

Within the Regional HRD ecosystem in Southeast Asia, there are four central components of the meso dimension: educational institutions, professional networks, international organizations and consultant networks, and family and peer networks. Together, these components make up the networks and actors that "formulate and implement" HRD policy and practice in the region (Garavan et al., 2019, p. 263). Embedded within the previously discussed macro dimension, these institutions and networks have a more direct impact on HRD practice and policy in many ways than macro components like culture, governments, and ASEAN.

4.1 Educational Institutions

The first component of this dimension is educational institutions. Educational institutions, especially those in higher education, play a key role in Regional HRD, as they "train the skilled work force necessary for economic development" (Sugimura, 2012, p. 57). K-12 educational institutions, although relevant to a broader discussion of human capital development (Becker, 1993), are less relevant to HRD because they often lack a direct connection to workforce preparedness. In Southeast Asia, coordinating higher education programs to promote the development

O. S. Crocco, *Developing Human Resources in Southeast Asia*, Palgrave Macmillan Asian Business Series,
https://doi.org/10.1007/978-3-030-79697-6_4

of a regional workforce began before ASEAN, with the establishment of the Association of Southeast Asian Institutions of Higher Learning in 1956 and the South-East Asian Ministers of Education Organization (SEAMEO) in 1965. While these initial efforts made progress in the regional coordination of the higher education sector, it was not until 1992, with the establishment of the ASEAN Free Trade Area (AFTA), that the governments of ASEAN member countries were motivated to mobilize higher education to track with labor market needs. This connection between higher education and industry, albeit often tenuous, is the main way in which higher education institutions directly influence Regional HRD. The more that a region's countries tie their economic fates together, the more that the region uses mechanisms such as higher education to facilitate integrated economic development.

The ASEAN Economic Community Blueprint 2025 articulates the connection between HRD and higher education, stating that one of its purposes is to:

> Foster robust productivity growth through innovation, technology and human resource development, and intensified regional research and development that is designed for commercial application to increase ASEAN's competitive edge in moving the region up the global value chains (GVCs) into higher technology and knowledge-intensive manufacturing and services industries. (ASEAN, 2015a, p. 2)

4.1.1 Universities and Regional HRD

At present, there are over 200 universities within Southeast Asia that interface with governments, organizations, and individuals in a variety of ways that influence and implement Regional HRD. The value that universities place on innovation and commercialization in their connection to government and the private sector (Gachie, 2020) makes higher education all the more relevant to Regional HRD. Universities also function as a source of local knowledge creation that is useful for subsidiaries as they seek to develop human resources locally (Garavan et al., 2019).

Many large corporations have entered the higher education space in Southeast Asia either by creating corporate universities or cultivating partnerships with universities to ensure that their graduates receive the knowledge and skills necessary to be effective in their organization (Crocco et al., 2017). Many large corporations also utilize local training schools to develop their employees such as Hanoi Production Services Import–Export Joint Stock Company, or Haprosimex, which relies on training institutes in Ho Chi Minh City for competency development (Park et al., 2017). And large corporations such as Indonesia's PT Petrosea Tbk offer HRD-related training programs for supervisors and senior managers in collaboration with the University of Prasetiya Mulya just southwest of Jakarta (Petrosea, 2019). Similarly, the Singaporean-based marine engineering firm Sembcorp Marine, which includes operations in Indonesia, has run a leadership development program in partnership with Singapore Management University (Sembcorp Marine, 2019). This is part of a larger trend of universities in the region becoming more entrepreneurial (Chao, 2018).

Universities also offer training in various topics that support capacity development in the region. For example, Charmondusit et al. (2012) discuss a problem-based training program on "industrial ecology and environment" developed by Mahidol University in Thailand and offered to participants from a variety of countries in the region (p. 30).

Other projects include Asifood, a 3-year Erasmus + Program funded by the European Commission, which collaborated with universities in three Southeast Asian countries (Cambodia, Thailand, and Vietnam) and four European countries (Austria, Belgium, Italy, and France) (Anal et al., 2020). The project sought to build capacity within higher education contexts and provided training on food safety and quality. The focus of the program was engaging with stakeholders and preparing the food industry for ASEAN integration (Anal et al., 2020). Given that the Southeast Asian countries were all ASEAN member countries, the program was informed by the ASEAN Food Safety Policy (ASEAN, 2016), working with the member countries to meet the principles outlined in that policy document (Anal et al., 2020).

Higher education in Southeast Asia is also becoming increasingly involved in community development and social responsibility (Symaco & Tee, 2019). Initiatives and centers like the Centre for Global Sustainability Studies of the Universiti Sains Malaysia have offered disaster management training courses in Vietnam, Lao PDR, and Cambodia (Ahmad Shabudin et al., 2017).

Universities also provide students with the soft skills and competencies necessary for the Southeast Asian workforce. In a needs analysis of Indonesian engineering students (Araminta & Halimi, 2015), an HR director of a multinational enterprise operating in seven Southeast Asian countries identified applied and practical English language skills as a key need, especially as they relate to the ASEAN Economic Community. Other tertiary education options such as ESL allow students to develop important competencies. In Malaysia, one teacher has used debate as a method for building soft skills and lifelong learning (Aclan et al., 2016). The need for soft skill development is only growing as technological advancements automate away jobs that rely on manual tasks (Ra et al., 2019).

While educational institutions contribute to HRD generally via workforce development and training, more universities are beginning to offer undergraduate and graduate programs in the field of HRD. Two such examples are the National Institute for Development Administration (NIDA) in Thailand and the Universiti Teknologi Malaysia (McLean & Akaraborworn, 2015). NIDA publishes an academic journal, the *Human Resource and Organizational Development Journal*, that focuses solely on HRD research. In a 2014 survey of specific HR trends in Southeast Asia, Akaraborworn identified corporate social responsibility, performance management, and organization development as the top three.

While many of the universities in Southeast Asia are traditional institutions of higher learning, there are also innovative organizations such as Thailand's Sukhothai Thammathirat Open University (STOU) and Ramkhamheang University, which are low-cost distance education universities, also called open universities, available to students all over the country (Crocco, 2018). As a result of their accessibility and low cost, these open universities enroll hundreds of thousands of students each year.

A key initiative after AFTA set the stage for regional economic integration was the ASEAN University Network (AUN), which was established in 1995 and now includes 30 Southeast Asian universities from all 10 ASEAN member states. The AUN facilitates collaboration in the region in five areas: curriculum and learning strategies, quality assurance, skill enhancement, research, and networking platforms (AUN, 2017). However, organizations such as AUN are often fraught with inefficiency and lack of agency. This lack of agency is exemplified by its attempt to promote a unified system of quality assurance (QA). The AUN established the AUN Quality Assurance (AUN-QA) network as a means of standardization, yet it has had only moderate success in ensuring the quality of higher education (Umemiya, 2008). Furthermore, the AUN-QA network is not the only mechanism in the region that seeks to regulate the industry. Most countries and universities in the region are influenced by a variety of QA mechanisms, such as the SEAMEO Regional Centre for Higher Education and Development, the Asia-Pacific Quality Network, and the International Network for Quality Assurance Agencies in Higher Education (Pitiyanuwat, 2011). Thus, many universities in Southeast Asia are overburdened with managing QA and must satisfy both national and external standards, such as those mentioned above. As a result, many of them struggle in international rankings (see Table 4.1).

Despite this issue, the quality of universities in Southeast Asia has been improving internationally in recent years. The four most popular world university rankings are provided by QS Top Universities (2021), which ranks 1187 universities; ShanghaiRanking (2020), which ranks 1000 universities; Times Higher Education (2021), which ranks 1526 universities; and the U.S. News & World Report (2021), which ranks 1678 universities. Universities in Southeast Asian countries appear a total of 150 times in these four rankings, although four countries (Cambodia, Lao PDR, Myanmar, and East Timor) do not have a single university listed. Of the Southeast Asian universities earning a high spot in the rankings, those from five countries—Singapore, Malaysia, Thailand, Indonesia, and Brunei—dominate, with two Singaporean universities, National University Singapore and Nanyang Technological University, appearing at the top of all four lists (see Table 4.2).

Table 4.1 Number of universities in each Southeast Asian country ranked

Southeast Asian country	*QS*	*ARWU*	*THE*	*US*
Singapore	3	4	2	4
Malaysia	21	5	15	12
Thailand	10	4	17	11
Indonesia	11	0	9	2
Philippines	4	0	2	2
Vietnam	4	0	3	2
Brunei	2	0	1	0
Cambodia	0	0	0	0
Lao PDR	0	0	0	0
Myanmar	0	0	0	0
Timor-Leste	0	0	0	0

Sources QS Top Universities (2021), U.S. News and World Report (2021), Times Higher Education (2021) and ShanghaiRanking Consultancy (2020)

Table 4.2 Top three universities in each Southeast Asian country according to international rankings

Ranking				*University*	*Country*
QS	*US*	*THE*	*ARWU*		
11	32	25	80	National University of Singapore	Singapore
13	38	47	91	Nanyang Technological University	Singapore
59	205	301–350	301–400	Universiti Malaya	Malaysia
252	511	601–800	401–500	Mahidol University	Thailand
142	580	601–800	501–600	Universiti Sains Malaysia	Malaysia
187	468	601–800	601–700	Universiti Teknologi Malaysia	Malaysia
208	516	601–800	701–800	Chulalongkorn University	Thailand
254	–	351–400	–	Universiti Brunei Darussalam	Brunei
305	831	801–1000	–	Universitas Indonesia	Indonesia
254	1304	1000+	–	Gadjah Mada University	Indonesia
313	–	1000+	–	Bandung Institute of Technology	Indonesia
350	–	–	–	Universiti Teknologi Brunei	Brunei
396	1217	401–500	–	University of the Philippines	Philippines
511–520	769	–	–	Singapore Management University	Singapore
601–650	856	1000+	901–1000	Chiang Mai University	Thailand
601–650	–	–	–	Ateneo de Manila University	Philippines
801–1000	949	801–1000	–	Vietnam National University, Hanoi	Vietnam
801–1000	1271	1000+	–	Vietnam National University, HCMC	Vietnam
801–1000	–	1000+	–	De La Salle University	Philippines
1000+	–	1000+	–	Hanoi University of Science & Tech	Vietnam

Sources QS Top Universities (2021), U.S. News and World Report (2021), Times Higher Education (2021) and ShanghaiRanking Consultancy (2020)

The greatest challenge facing higher education in Southeast Asia has been the need to import human resources to cover its existing skills gaps as well as a "brain drain" from lower-income countries such as Cambodia, where faculty are overworked and under-compensated (Keo & Jun, 2016, p. 617). Faculty development has been an important priority for many Southeast Asian countries, with Singapore, Malaysia, and Vietnam leading the way (Phuong et al., 2015). That said, in most cases, faculty development has not been as valued by leaders and many faculty members have struggled with balancing their various administrative roles (Phuong et al., 2015). To address this issue, Phuong et al. (2015) recommend that Southeast Asian universities set up centers on campus devoted to developing faculty skills in research and teaching and use more effective forms of faculty evaluation to better understand needs and areas of improvement.

4.1.2 Technical and Vocational Education and Training

Technical and vocational education and training (TVET), which typically falls under tertiary education, also contributes to Regional HRD broadly, especially as it pertains to achieving the goals of the ASEAN Economic Community (Bai & Paryono, 2019; Yoto, 2016). Whereas traditional higher education at a four-year university is meant to bring about a more rounded and general education that could apply to a variety of contexts over one's career in the dynamic market economy, TVET offers highly specified "job-relevant skills" (Tilak, 2003, p. 673). In some Southeast Asian contexts, TVET is an alternative to traditional higher education (e.g., the Philippines) whereas in others it can also be a stepping stone to higher education (e.g., Indonesia, Myanmar).

While some might view TVET as related more closely to national HRD (McLean, 2021), TVET is so interconnected in the Regional HRD ecosystem, that some Southeast Asian countries see value in supporting TVET systems in other countries as a means of supporting government and business activities. For example, the Singapore-Myanmar Vocational Training Institute (SMVTI) is a collaboration between Singapore and Myanmar, based in Yangon, that is overseen by the Institute of Technical Education in Singapore and offers training in 10 occupations (Bai & Wu, 2019). SMVTI has memorandums of understanding with a variety of companies in Singapore and Myanmar to ensure that its training is aligned with industry needs (SMVTI, n.d.).

The value of TVET from a regional perspective can also be seen in Vietnam where vocational educational institutions such as those in the garment and textile industry play an important role in skill development (Quang et al., 2020). Vietnam, like all countries in Southeast Asia, is competing against the regional workforce in areas like agriculture, manufacturing, and tourism where TVET contributes to competitive advantage

(McLean, 2021). While Vietnam has made strides in realizing its recent Law on Vocational Education adopted in 2014 (ILO, n.d.) that would bring about greater autonomy and reformed policies for TVET, many challenges remain (McLean, 2021). These include but are not limited to "adapting the [TVET] system to technological developments" and "poor ratio of skilled workers working in the sector" (Caggiano, 2018, para 8).

As mentioned in the previous chapter, governance and implementation of TVET vary country-by-country depending on the unique historical development of education systems and current political priorities (Tilak, 2003). In the Philippines, for example, the government's Technical Education and Skills Development Authority runs TVET in the country. In Indonesia, TVET is governed by a set of ministries depending on the nature of TVET. The Ministry of Education and Culture oversees general TVET, which includes teacher training, the Ministry of Research, Technology and Higher Education oversees specialized TVET within polytechnics, and the Ministry of Manpower and Transmigration oversees TVET within national training centers (Triyono & Moses, 2019).

In terms of implementation, in countries like Vietnam and Brunei, governments take near-complete responsibility for the implementation of TVET; however, in countries such as Cambodia, Myanmar, and Indonesia, private TVET institutes and NGOs also play a role in delivering TVET (Bai & Paryono, 2019). At least in the case of Cambodia and Myanmar, the reliance on private providers of TVET was useful given the limited resources and government priorities for education generally.

One of the most pressing frontiers of TVET in Southeast Asia is its relationship with information and communications technology (ICT), in particular in its ability to bring about "digital inclusion" (OECD, 2019, p.121). Using HRD to develop digital literacy generally to close the digital divide is one of the five strategic areas of the ASEAN ICT Masterplan 2020 (ASEAN, 2015b). In their final report of the master plan, ASEAN (2021) describes the development of the ASEAN ICT Skills Standards that were created across five skill areas as well as the way HRD can be utilized to develop ICT skills in the region. Regional coordination around TVET is not limited to ASEAN involvement. For example, the Regional Association of Vocational and Technical Education in Asia (RAVTE), which was founded in Chiang Mai, Thailand, supports TVET at the national and regional levels in East and Southeast Asia through an annual conference, strategic meetings, workshops, and knowledge sharing (RAVTE, n.d.). Their efforts focus on green TVET for the future of sustainable and environmentally friendly work, TVET in an age of digitalization and automation, and TVET that meets the needs of private and public stakeholders (RAVTE, n.d.). RAVTE as a whole is well-positioned to make an impact regionally on TVET and to help coordinate national systems, especially because the top strategic objective in their Strategy and Action Plan of 2019–2023 is to increase harmonization with ASEAN's Qualification Reference Framework (Schröder, 2019).

Individual countries have done creative programs with ICT and TVET such as Singapore's SkillsFuture platform (SkillsFuture, n.d.). Designed "to encourage individual ownership of skills development and lifelong learning," SkillsFuture provides every Singaporean citizen over 25-years-old $500 to spend on courses offered through its TVET institutions (SkillsFuture, 2021, para 1). For example, someone could take an introductory course on 3D animation from Nanyang Polytechnic for $260 of their $500 or a course in strategic human resource planning offered by Singapore Human Resources Institute for $400 of their $500.

Whether through traditional higher education and TVET or more innovative online offerings in the future, there is a clear sense in the region that "quality education and training will remain a key public policy issue not only because of the need to address the mismatch between skills supply and demand, but also for ASEAN economies to remain competitive in the future" (Basu Das, 2015, p. 56). This means that appropriate investment and regional strategy to enhance these efforts will be vital to the region's future.

4.2 Professional Networks

Another component of the meso dimension of the Regional HRD ecosystem is comprised of the many professional HRD networks in the region. Professional networks are relationships that are established for business reasons, or that focus on a specific career, profession, or topic such as HRD. These include large-scale international professional networks such as the Society for Human Resource Management (SHRM) and smaller, national, or regional professional networks like the Singapore Human Resources Institute (SHRI) or the ASEAN Confederation of Employers (ACE) Professional networks influence policy, practice, and research related to HRD at the organizational, national, and regional levels. In particular, these networks influence what is considered best practice in HRD at the organizational level (Kim et al., 2017). Networks also shed light on the different but complementary concepts of HRD and human resource management (HRM) (see Chapter 1). Many professional networks in this dimension have to deal with HRM more than with HRD. Even the conceptualizations of HRM and HRD can be ambiguous, often overlapping depending on a country's or organization's purposes. Even though many of these professional networks support Regional HRD at the organizational and individual levels through HRM, they are still a vital component of Regional HRD more broadly.

Professional networks exist at various levels, such as international, regional, and national. The large-scale professional organizations such as the Academy of Human Resource Development (AHRD) and SHRM represent the international level, while the Asia Pacific Federation of Human Resource Management (APFHRM) represents a regional network. These three actors, which support different areas related to human resources that directly influence Regional HRD, are of particular note given their influence on the profession and practice.

SHRM and AHRD support the field in Southeast Asia, albeit largely indirectly. SHRM, a U.S.-based HRM organization, has influenced how organizations around the world approach the development of their human resources, especially MNCs with Americans working in HR. SHRM holds an annual conference, publishes books and resources related to HRM, and oversees the certification of individuals as SHRM Certified Professionals or SHRM Senior Certified Professionals (SHRM, n.d.). SHRM also has a foundation that has funded research such as that conducted by De Ciere and Bardoel (2009). SHRM has investigated work-life management in China and Southeast Asia, finding that MNCs influence local HRM practices in Southeast Asian subsidiaries.

An organization like SHRM is more practitioner-oriented; however, AHRD takes a more academic approach to the region. AHRD was founded in 1993, after breaking away from what is now the Association for Talent Development, to pursue research in the field. As a result, AHRD holds annual conferences and includes an Asian chapter, which has held international academic conferences in Thailand (2018), Vietnam (2019), and Malaysia (2021). AHRD also provides publishing outlets for HRD scholars through its four sponsored HRD journals: *Human Resource Development International*, *Advances in Developing Human Resources*, *Human Resource Development Review*, and *Human Resource Development Quarterly*.

APFHRM is a regional organization that supports the creation of national-level associations. Founded in 1977, APFHRM now includes 17 members in Asia and the Pacific, five of which are Southeast Asian countries (Malaysia, the Philippines, Singapore, Thailand, and Vietnam). The vision of APFHRM is to "advance the standing of the HR and people management profession within the region" by the exchange of information, research, and best practices (2018, p. 3). Its four objectives are to serve as the "umbrella organization of all human resource institutes" in the Asia-Pacific, to improve the quality of HRM, to encourage Asian-Pacific countries as they develop their own HR-related associations, and to guide member countries as they develop the profession in their own country (APFHRM, 2018, p. 7). APFHRM is one of five regional members of the World Federation of People Management Associations along with the European Association of People Management, the Interamerican Federation of Human Resource Management, the North American Human Resource Management Association, and the African Human Resources Confederation. APFHRM provides a clear example of how a professional network at the regional level connects to both the national and the global level.

APFHRM supports the professional organizations in each of the represented Southeast Asian countries, which includes the Malaysian Institute of Human Resource Management (MIHRM), the Personnel Management Association of Thailand (PMAT), the Personnel Management Association of Philippines (PMAP), the aforementioned SHRI, and the Human Resources Association of Vietnam. Several of these associations publish their own practitioner-oriented magazines to share knowledge and develop the profession nationally. For example, PMAT publishes a bi-quarterly magazine, *HR Magazine*; PMAP publishes a monthly magazine, *People Manager*; and SHRI publishes a bi-monthly publication, *Human Capital*.

Another regional professional organization is the ASEAN Confederation of Employers (ACE), which was founded in 1978. Similar to APFHRM, ACE is comprised of national organizations, namely, the Cambodian Federation of Employers and Business Associations, Employers' Association of Indonesia, Lao National Chamber of Commerce and Industry, Malaysian Employers Federation, Employers Confederation of the Philippines, Singapore National Employers Federation, and

Employers Confederation of Thailand. To achieve its mission to "safeguard employers' interests" and bring about "the most conducive environment to enhance productivity, efficiency, and competitiveness" (ACE, 2020, para 1), ACE holds forums and shares resources, working to influence policy and practice in business, some of which is related to HRD. For example, ACE (2021) has published a policy brief on women migrant workers that shared data on the value that they can bring to organizations in Southeast Asia. The report also recommended providing gender sensitivity training and using more women migrant workers as trainers (ACE, 2021).

Qualification frameworks are also often connected to professional networks as they mutually influence one another. In addition to AUN-QA, the QA mechanism mentioned in the last section, and the ASEAN Qualifications Reference Framework (AQRF), Southeast Asian countries use other frameworks that often have implications for Regional HRD. For example, Blackburn and Rosen (1993) found that firms that won the Malcolm Baldrige National Quality Award (MBNQA) developed human resources in ways that promoted Total Quality Management (TQM). Influenced by MBNQA, Thailand and Singapore each have Quality Awards for organizations that meet business excellence framework criteria. The criteria for these awards include policies and practices related to HRD such as organizational learning, leadership, and management (National Institute of Standards and Technology, n.d.). Similar to Thailand and Singapore, the Philippines has the Philippines National Quality Award and Vietnam has the Vietnam Quality Award. While not officially affiliated with MBNQA, both awards also involve training and certifications. Quality awards can dictate Regional HRD policy and practice by influencing the HRD-related business dimensions of organizations.

In the professional network space, there has also been a recent movement away from using the phrase "human resources" and toward using the phrase "human development" (Aubrey, 2020). The ASEAN Human Development Organization founded by Bob Aubrey and Southeast Asian colleagues builds on the unique cultural, political, and economic positionality of Southeast Asian countries and synthesizes a new model for human development in the region based on ethics, changes in technology and job design, and shifts from a national to a regional perspective. The ASEAN Human Development Organization offers three levels of certification for individuals and two types of accreditation for organizations for those wanting to align themselves and their organizations with this human development approach.

Finally, HR-related magazines and websites play a tangential role in shaping discourse related to Regional HRD. For example, there are HRD- and HR-related magazines and websites such as Human Resources Online (n.d.) and ASEANHR (n.d, and Prospects (n.d.), which is a Southeast Asia-based company that publishes an online resource center on "careers, education and personal development – ensuring ASEAN students, graduates and young professionals have access to the best tools, opportunities and expert advice before making a decision on their education and career direction" (Prospects, n.d., para 2). There are larger, more comprehensive websites such as HRM Asia (n.d.), which is headquartered in Singapore and offers an HR leadership series of webinars and case studies, and resources across a variety of HRD-related topics.

4.3 International Organizations and Consultant Networks

Southeast Asian cities like Bangkok, Singapore, Manila, Kuala Lumpur, and Ho Chi Min City serve as international hubs for multinational corporations (MNCs) as well as subsidiaries of U.S., European, and other Asian corporations. Considering the status of many of the ASEAN states as emerging economies, many have also relied on networks of consultants and expatriates to support the development of HRD policy and practice. Among MNCs operating in Southeast Asian countries, it has long been known that vertical linkages between the MNC headquarters and local subsidiaries are possible under certain conditions (Lim & Pang, 1982). Furthermore, "International firms contribute to integration because their cross-border investments in affiliates and their joint ventures and strategic alliances are trade promoting" (Dobson, 1997, p. 7). This component of the meso dimension of the Regional HRD ecosystem is often overlooked, but international organizations and networks of consultants "play a major networking and knowledge transfer role in organizations" (Garavan et al., 2019, p. 263).

For this meso component in particular, given the diversity and breadth of organizations and consultant networks that influence Regional HRD, it would be impossible to list them all and describe the ways in which they influence the Regional HRD ecosystem. However, it is worth presenting several exemplars to provide researchers and practitioners with a sense of the power of this component of the Regional HRD ecosystem.

Organizations such as the Economic Research Institute for ASEAN and East Asia (ERIA) have long shaped policy and research related to HRD in Southeast Asia. What began as a collaboration between the ASEAN Economic Ministers and Japan's Ministry of Economy, Trade, and Industry in 2006 has expanded to a full-fledged research institute that provides books, policy briefs, and white papers for policymakers in the region. One of their core areas is Education, Training, and Human Capital, in which they publish research such as Dang and Dang's (2020) paper on "The role of innovation in skill development: Evidence from small and medium-sized enterprises in Viet Nam" and Yusef et al.'s (2019) policy brief on "Human resources development in Indonesia – Towards 2045." ERIA also has HRD-related programs such as its Capacity Building Programme, which even amidst the pandemic has used online to support HRD in the region including its recent e-workshop on e-commerce offered to Cambodian government officials (ERIA, 2020).

Other significant contributors include the Asian Development Bank (ADB), the International Labor Organization (ILO), and the World Bank (WB). ADB carries out development projects and publishes research related to HRD in individual Southeast Asian countries as well as the region as a whole. For example, in 2021, ADB published a series of reports concerning the benefits of skill development projects in countries such as Cambodia (ADB, 2021a) and the Philippines (ADB, 2021b).WB has also been working with national-level organizations such as Thailand's National Economic and Social Development Council in conjunction with the ASEAN High Level Meeting on Human Capital Development to bring about "a set of common, yet context-adapted, policy directions" (Devdiscourse, 2019, para 3).

Similarly, ILO has backed publications such as Aring (2015), which analyzes how HRD in ASEAN member countries can be supported to align national and regional priorities. Similarly, the WB has not only influenced policy and research in the region, but it has also collaborated with ASEAN. Its influence in the Regional HRD ecosystem is shown in the WB (2013) report on ASEAN integration. Ford et al. (2018) have pointed out that the ILO as a development actor has had an "unusually interventionist approach" in countries like Myanmar, which has allowed it to conduct activities, with the government's support, related to "promoting fundamental principles and rights at work, strengthening employers' and workers' organizations and labor market institutions, and enhancing employment opportunities and social protection" (pp. 89–90).

In addition to these large international organizations and development banks, there are also international non-governmental organizations (INGOs) that influence the Regional HRD ecosystem. For example, Education Development Center (EDC) based in Boston, MA won funding from the United States Agency for International Development (USAID) for an innovative project entitled the "USAID-Lower Mekong Initiative Connecting the Mekong through Education and Training (USAID-LMI COMET)" (EDC, n.d.). Partners in the project included corporations such as Cisco, Amazon, Intel and Google, and universities such as Mahidol University (Thailand), University of Technology Yatanarpon Cyber City (Myanmar), Institute of Technology Cambodia, Hanoi University of Science and Technology (Vietnam), and the National University of Laos. Given this project's regional focus within Southeast Asia and its relevance to Regional HRD, it is worth expanding on further.

Motivated by the 2015 ASEAN Economic Community and the need for HRD to meet the labor market needs of regional workforce integration, this 12.4 million USD project sought to promote skill development as well as alignment between education and training institutions and industry partners in Cambodia, Lao PDR, Myanmar, Thailand, and Vietnam (EDC, 2019).USAID-LMI COMET collaborated with Mahidol University to carry out a set of three labor market assessment studies. Then, a network of universities served as advisors and helped develop and implement a framework for post-secondary education and training interventions that would serve the HRD needs of workers in those countries.

To support sustainable economic growth and improved capacity that could go to scale, the project built a regional Mekong Skills2Work (MS2W) Network, made up of 12 universities and vocational colleges that the project referred to as Mekong Learning Centers (MLCs) (EDC, 2019). The professional development component of the MS2W network included a sourcebook that gave instructors "standards-based toolkits" based on needed twenty-first century skills identified in the labor market assessments as relevant and necessary for workers in those areas. Trainers from all over the Lower Mekong subregion became certified as Master Trainers through in person workshops and innovative online courses. Not only did these trainers become trained in facilitating skill development to meet industry needs, they also learned how to model a "student-centered learning experience" (EDC, 2019, p. 19). The project also facilitated several innovation challenges where teams competed in a project-based tasks using teamwork and critical thinking skills to solve complex questions.

The project worked with MLCs to strengthen their partnerships with local industry. Local industry engaged with the educational institutions in six ways: "providing input to curriculum, sponsoring events, providing technology, providing services, providing scholarships, and providing internships and jobs" (EDC, 2019, p. 27). Overall, the project fostered over 700 partnerships with multinational corporations.

Perhaps most compelling in this project was its ability to scale, exemplified in its adoption nation-wide in Myanmar and included in 20 universities led by the University of Technology (Yatanarpon Cyber City). Given how centralized the education system is in Myanmar generally (Zobrist & McCormick, 2017), a project such as this has a lot of potential to improve the quality of the system and connection to workforce needs. The fact that it facilitated a bottom-up approach in a more top-down educational system, shows its unique contribution to HRD.

While funding agencies such as USAID typically focus on national projects, the USAID-LMI COMET project represents an acknowledgment that regional projects among countries as integrated as those in Southeast Asia are imperative as a result of regional integration. In fact, according to the project's final report, "[b]eing a regional project drove many of the decisions that shaped the project's approach" (EDC, 2019, p. 17). This meant that EDC could not simply introduce an educational curriculum that would fit into the cultural and political environment of all five countries without it being relegated to an extracurricular activity. It also meant that the project did not work directly with national governments. To maintain its legitimacy and effectiveness as a curricular-based project that would fit within the national standards of the five countries it shifted to its bottom-up approach (EDC, 2019). The regional nature of this project, among other reasons (e.g., geo-politics and USAID's limited work in China), is also perhaps related to why Yunnan Province, China was not included in this project despite being considered part of the Greater Mekong Subregion.

The Asia Foundation is another organization contributing to the Regional HRD ecosystem through policy and research. Recent reports such as "The future of work across ASEAN: Policy prerequisites for the fourth industrial revolution" (Asia Foundation, 2020) discuss the role that HRD plays in meeting market needs in various ASEAN member countries and how those countries can leverage HRD initiatives to meet the skilled labor demands of the future. There are also think tanks like the Singapore Institute of International Affairs, which is an independent organization that offers commentary related to economics and global citizenship in the region, which often includes implications for Regional HRD.

While ASEAN was mentioned in Chapter 3 as a part of the macro dimension of the Regional HRD ecosystem given its influence on so many aspects of HRD throughout the region, it could easily have gone in this chapter as part of the meso dimension. While ASEAN is the most integrated and influential regional organization in Southeast Asia, other regional organizations overlap with ASEAN in many regards and make additional contributions to HRD in the region.

Take, for example, the Asian Partnership for the Development of Human Resources in Rural Areas (AsiaDHRRA) made up of 11 Asian countries, eight of which are Southeast Asian (Cambodia, Indonesia, Lao PDR, the Philippines, Malaysia, Myanmar, Thailand, and Vietnam) along with East Asian countries of Japan, South Korea, and Taiwan, AsiaDHRRA began addressing HRD needs of rural communities with the Human Rural Resources in Asia Workshop held in Thailand in 1974 (AsiaDHRRA, n.d.-a). Each member country has its own chapter of AsiaDHRRA, e.g., LaoDHRRA, which goes by the Sustainable Agriculture & Environment Development Association (SAEDA), which works on "improving [vulnerable communities'] capacity and awareness" regarding sustainable agriculture (SAEDA, n.d.). The overarching AsiaDHRRA works with the chapters of the 11 member countries to achieve its overarching vision of rural communities becoming "just, free, prosperous, living in peace and working in solidarity towards self-reliance," AsiaDHRRA (n.d.-b, para 1). The main mechanism that AsiaDHRRA uses to work toward its vision is HRD-related initiatives, particularly as it relates to rural people's organizations or RPOs and organizational development.

One key project of AsiaDHRRA has been the Regional Cooperation to Empower Rural Development Organizations in Asia project, which was supported by the European Union and exclusively focused on the capacity building and organizational development in RPOs in the eight Southeast Asian member countries. This project focused on regional capacity building themes of financial sustainability through "social enterprise and project development" and policy advocacy and localization of sustainable development goals (AsiaDHRRA, 2021, slide 8). To this end, the project trained 2457 leaders and second-liners of RPOs and civil society organizations. Part of this involves regional information systems that would be able to serve organizations throughout the region in an ongoing fashion (AsiaDHRRA, 2021). Here is another illustration of an international organization working collaboratively in the region to develop human resources to a certain end.

A key component of this dimension is also the role that consultant networks play in the ecosystem. There are a vast number of large, international management consulting firms with operations in Southeast Asian countries. For Example, Deloitte (n.d.) has offices in all 11 Southeast Asian countries, McKinsey (n.d.) has offices in seven, Boston Consulting Group (n.d.) has offices in six, Bain and Co. (n.d.) has offices in five, and Kearney (n.d.) has offices in four. In some cases, these organizations have had a longstanding presence in Southeast Asia such as Deloitte, which began its operations in Thailand in 1939 (Deloitte, 2019). While management consulting is not always directly related to HRD policy and practice, there are often projects where local or international consultants as part of these firms support organizations in issues that involve issues of training and development, leadership development, or people management. They also offer reports and research related to the region that can inform HRD policy and practice. For example, in Mckinsey's report "Bringing Industry 4.0 to life for companies in Southeast Asia," Lin (2017) talks about the role of training and skill development in regional growth.

4.4 Family and Peer Networks

The last component in this dimension is represented by the networks of family and peers that shape HRD policy and practice in the region. These networks and relationships are found within organizational hierarchies, between organizations, and in personal relationships (Theingi et al., 2008). Given the general importance that social networks have in the Southeast Asian context (Chua & Wellman, 2015a), family and peer networks make up an important influence on the Regional HRD ecosystem. Even early ASEAN publications such as *Preparing workersfor changes in the labor market: The ASEAN Experience* highlights the fact that:

> The employment relationship is not simply a market or contractual transaction. There are also social and cultural dimensions involved, since people develop lifetime networks, friendships and partnerships in the workplace.

> A comprehensive understanding of the dimensions which enable decent, humane and productive work should consider not only the business aspects, i.e. product and labour markets, but also social relations. (ASEAN, 2001, p. 38)

Family and intra-familial relationships are incredibly important in the Southeast Asian context as they provide "a continuous, flued process of negotiations, contracts and exchange – whether altruistic, reciprocal, unequal or oppressive – within the context of broader political, economic and social change" (Yeoh & Huang, 2018, p. 173).

HRD practices such as training and mentoring occur in family business contexts that build skills and knowledge, in particular for the successor(s) and build the social networks that influence the continuity and success of the organization (Lee, 2008). Within the family network setting, the "acquisition of appropriate entrepreneurial knowledge, motivation, and identification resulting from training, work experience, and socialization respectively, improve the cognitive understanding, self-efficacy, and psychological readiness to be an effective successor" (Lee, 2008, p. 267). In a study of over 500 Malaysian micro-enterprises, family support in terms of a variety of methods including HRD partially mediates management and intrinsic motivation and fully mediates business opportunities for those entrepreneurs (Zakaria & Halim, 2016).

Given the large proportion of ethnic Chinese in Southeast Asia and the importance of family networks in Chinese business contexts, the cultural concept of *guanxi*, or "networks of useful personal relationships," is common throughout Southeast Asia (Menkhoff & Labig, 1996, p. 131; Chua & Wellman, 2015b). In a study of social capital in Southeast Asian businesses (Theingi et al., 2008), found that social relationships contributed to skill development. Garavan et al. (2019) rightly put family and peer networks in the meso dimension of the international HRD ecosystem; however, in the regional context of Southeast Asia, it could be argued that given the closeness of family and peers to workers, employees, and local units, that they fit better at the micro level of the Southeast Asian Regional HRD ecosystem. That said, given their more common role as connectors and facilitators and not central actors themselves, it is still likely most appropriate to place family and peer networks in the meso dimension while recognizing that there is often overlap and instances of direct impact of family and peers on HRD.

Bibliography

Aclan, E., Abd Aziz, N. H., & Valdez, N. P. (2016). Debate as pedagogical tool to develop soft skills in EFL/ESL classroom: A qualitative case study. *Pertanika Journal of Social Sciences & Humanities, 24*(1), 213–240.

Ahmad Shabudin, A. F., Azhar, S. N. F. S., & Ng, T. F. (2017). Learning lab on disaster risk management for sustainable development (DRM-SD): An evaluation. *International Journal of Climate Change Strategies and Management, 9*(5), 600–625. https://doi.org/10.1108/IJCCSM-08-2016-0114.

Akaraborworn, C. (2014). Comparative study of HR trends in ASEAN 2014–2015 [In Thai]. *HROD Journal, 6*(2), 4–41. http://www.hrd.nida.ac.th/shrdjournal/image/2.%20For%20Web%202_2557/5.%20comparative%20study.pdf.

Anal, A. K., Waché, Y., Louzier, V., Laurent, R., Mens, F., Avalllone, S., Mahakarnchanakul, W., Udompijitkul, P., Tantikitti, C., Nguyen, T. B. T., Thao, P. P., Nguyen, T. M. T., Nguyen, H. M. X., Thong, K., Seingheng, H., Schleining, G., Linder, L. F., Scippo, M.-L., & Guidi, A. (2020). AsiFood and its output and prospects: An Erasmus+ project on capacity building in food safety and quality for South-East Asia. *Food Control, 109*, 1–6. https://doi.org/10.1016/j.foodcont.2019.106913.

Araminta, L. D. W., & Halimi, S. S. (2015). ASEAN Economic Community 2015: Needs analysis of Universitas Indonesia's engineering students. *Indonesia Journal of Applied Linguistics, 5*(1), 10–17. https://doi.org/10.17509%2Fijal.v5i1.841.

Aring, M. (2015). *ASEAN Economic Community 2015: Enhancing competitiveness and employability through skill development*. https://www.ilo.org/wcmsp5/groups/public/---asia/---ro-bangkok/documents/publication/wcms_344796.pdf.

ASEAN Confederation of Employers. (2020). *Mission and objectives*. http://aseanemployers.com/ace_website/mission-objectives-of-the-asean-confederation-of-employers/.

ASEAN Confederation of Employers. (2021). *The untapped power of women migrant workers in ASEAN: A business case for gender equality and empowerment in the work*. http://www.aseanemployers.com/ace_platform/assets/uploads/resources/60.pdf.

ASEAN HR. (n.d.). *Home*. https://aseanhr.org/.

ASEAN University Network. (n.d.). *History and background*. http://aunsec.org/ourhistory.php.

ASEAN University Network. (2017). *AUN Strategic Focus 2017–2021*. http://aunsec.org/pdf/AUN_Focus_2017-2021_For_POs_Planning.pdf.

Asia Foundation. (2020). *The future of work across ASEAN: Policy prerequisites for the fourth industrial revolution*. https://asiafoundation.org/wp-content/uploads/2020/02/The-Future-of-Work-Across-ASEAN_full.pdf.

Asia Pacific Federation of Human Resource Management. (2018). *Asia Pacific Federation of Human Resource Management (APFHRM) handbook*. http://apfhrm.com/docs/APFHRM%20handbook%202018.pdf.

Asian Development Bank. (2021a). *Reaping the benefits of Industry 4.0 through skills development in Cambodia*. https://www.adb.org/sites/default/files/publication/671726/benefits-industry-skills-development-cambodia.pdf.

Asian Development Bank. (2021b). *Reaping the benefits of Industry 4.0 through skills development in the Philippines*. https://www.adb.org/sites/default/files/publication/671881/benefits-industry-skills-development-philippines.pdf.

Asian Partnership for the Development of Human Resources in Rural Areas (AsiaDHRRA). (n.d.-a). *About AsiaDHRRA*. https://asiadhrra.org/about-us/our-history/.

Asian Partnership for the Development of Human Resources in Rural Areas (AsiaDHRRA). (n.d.-b). *Vision, mission and goals*. https://asiadhrra.org/about-us/vision-mission-and-goals/.

Asian Partnership for the Development of Human Resources in Rural Areas (AsiaDHRRA). (2021). *The regional cooperation to empower rural development organizations in Asia: Four years in brief*. https://asiadhrra.org/wp-content/uploads/2021/01/2-ReCoERDO-Milestones.pdf.

Association of Southeast Asian Nations. (2001). *Preparing workers for changes in the labour market: The ASEAN experience*. The ASEAN Secretariat.

Association of Southeast Asian Nations. (2015a). *ASEAN Economic Community Blueprint 2025*. https://www.asean.org/storage/2016/03/AECBP_2025r_FINAL.pdf.

Association of Southeast Asian Nations. (2015b). *The ASEAN ICT masterplan 2020*. https://asean.org/storage/images/2015/November/ICT/15b%20--%20AIM%202020_Publication_Final.pdf.

Association of Southeast Asian Nations. (2016). *ASEAN food safety policy*. https://asean.org/storage/2012/10/ASEAN-Food-Policy-030516_2.pdf.

Association of Southeast Asian Nations. (2021). *ASEAN ICT masterplan 2020: Final review*. https://asean.org/storage/V4.-Final-Draft-_-AIM 2020_Review_FInal_Draft_19Nov2020.pdf.

Aubrey, R. (2020). *Leading human development in ASEAN: Using management concepts from ASEAN countries to create an authentic model of human development*. McGraw Hill.

Bai, B., & Paryono (Eds.). (2019). *Vocational education and training in ASEAN member states: Current status and future development*. Springer.

Bai, B., & Wu, Q. (2019). Technical and vocational education and training in Myanmar. In B. Bai & Paryono (Eds.), *Vocational education and training in ASEAN member states: Current status and future development* (pp. 133–153). Springer. https://doi.org/10.1007/978-981-13-6617-8_6.

Bain & Company. (n.d.). *Global offices*. https://www.bain.com/about/offices/.

Basu Das, S. (2015). *The ASEAN economic community and beyond: Myths and realities*. ISEAS—Yusof Ishak Institute.

Becker, G. (1993). *Human capital: A theoretical and empirical analysis with special reference to education* (3rd ed.). The University of Chicago Press.

Blackburn, R., & Rosen, B. (1993). Total quality and human resources management: Lessons learned from Baldridge Award-winning companies. *Academy of Management Perspectives, 7*(3), 49–66. https://doi.org/10.5465/ame.1993.9411302347.

Boston Consulting Group. (n.d.). *BCG worldwide*. https://www.bcg.com/offices/default.

Caggiano, M. (2018, July 29). Current situation of technical and vocational education and training system in Vietnam. *TVET in Vietnam*. https://sustainableskills.org/tvet-system-in-vietnam/72932/.

Chao, R. Y. (2018). Entrepreneurial universities in ASEAN Nations: Insights from policy perspective. *Journal of Comparative & International Higher Education, 10*, 6–13.

Charmondusit, S., Bhaktikul, K., Arunlertaree, C., Wisawapipat, W., Rattanapan, C., & Charmondusit, K. (2012). Problem based training program on industrial ecology and environment for the sustainability management of industry. *Procedia—Social and Behavioral Sciences, 40*, 31–36. https://doi.org/10.1016/j.sbspro.2012.03.157.

Chua, V., & Wellman, B. (2015a). Social networks in East and Southeast Asia II: Labor migration, opportunity, social media, and well-being. *American Behavioral Scientist, 59*(9), 1055–1065.

Chua, V., & Wellman, B. (2015b). Social networks in East and Southeast Asia I: National characteristics, institutions, network capital, and guanxi. *American Behavioral Scientist, 59*(8), 903–913.

Crocco, O. S. (in press). The role of higher education in human resource development in Southeast Asia. In A. Bajrektarevic & R. Lao (Eds.), *Tomorrow ASEAN*. Nova Science Publishers.

Crocco, O. S. (2018). Thai higher education: Privatization and massification. In G. Fry (Ed.), *Education in Thailand* (pp. 223–255). Springer.

Crocco, O. S., Cseh, M., & Hemmapattawe, D. (2017). Corporate universities and corporation-university partnerships in Thailand: Complementing education in learning, leadership, and change. *Journal of International and Comparative Education, 6*(1), 17–31. https://doi.org/10.14425/JICE.2017.6.1.1732.

Dang, D. A., & Dang, V. A. (2020). *The role of innovation in skill development: Evidence from small and medium-sized enterprises in Viet Nam*. https://www.eria.org/uploads/media/discussion-papers/The-Role-of-Innovation-in-Skill-Development_Evidence-from-SMEs-in-Viet-Nam.pdf.

De Cieri, H., & Bardoel, E. A. (2009). What does "work-life management" mean in China and Southeast Asia for MNCs? *Community, Work & Family, 12*(2), 179–196. https://doi.org/10.1080/13668800902778959.

Deloitte. (n.d.). *Global office directory*. https://www2.deloitte.com/global/en/footerlinks/global-office-directory.html?icid=bottom_global-office-directory.

Deloitte. (2019). *Southeast Asia FY19 annual report*. https://www2.deloitte.com/sg/en/pages/about-deloitte/articles/sea-fy19-annual-review.html.

Devdiscourse. (2019, September 9). *ASEAN convened to discuss strategies for accelerating human capital development*. https://www.devdiscourse.com/article/headlines/664249-asean-convened-to-discuss-strategies-for-accelerating-human-capital-development.

Dobson, W. (1997). East Asian integration: Synergies between firm strategies and government policies. In W. Dobson & C. S. Yue (Eds.), *Multinationals and East Asian integration* (pp. 3–19). International Development Research Center.

Education Development Center. (n.d.). *USAID-Lower Mekong Initiative Connecting the Mekong through Education and Training (USAID-LMI COMET)*. https://edc.org/usaid-lmi-comet.

Education Development Center. (2019). *USAID-LMI connecting the Mekong through education and training: Final report September 2019*. Education Development Center.

Economic Research Institute for ASEAN and East Asia. (2020, October 8). *ERIA and the Cambodian Ministry of Commerce Kickstarts E-Commerce through online learning*. https://www.eria.org/database-and-programmes/eria-and-the-cambodian-ministry-of-commerce-kickstarts-e-commerce-through-online-learning/.

Feuer, H. N., & Hornidge, A. (2015). Higher education cooperation in ASEAN: Building towards integration or manufacturing consent? *Comparative Education, 51*(3), 327–352. https://doi.org/10.1080/03050068.2015.1031474.

Ford, M., Gillan, M., & Thein, H. H. (2018). The International Labour Organization as a development actor in Southeast Asia. In A. McGregor, L. Law, & F. Miller (Eds.), *Routledge handbook of Southeast Asian development* (pp. 85–95). Routledge.

Gachie, W. (2020). Higher education institutions, private sector and government collaboration for innovation within the framework of the Triple Helix Model. *African Journal of Science, Technology, Innovation and Development, 12*(2), 203–215. https://doi.org/10.1080/20421338.2019.1631120.

Garavan, T. N., McCarthy, A., & Carbery, R. (2019). An ecosystems perspective on international human resource development: A meta-synthesis of the literature. *Human Resource Development Review, 18*(2), 248–288. https://doi.org/10.1177/1534484319828865.

HRM Asia. (n.d.). *About us*. https://hrmasia.com/about-us/.
Human Resources Online. (n.d.). *About human resources*. https://www.humanresourcesonline.net/about-human-resources-online.
International Labour Organization. (n.d.). *Law on Vocational Education (Law No. 74/2014/QH13)*. https://www.ilo.org/dyn/natlex/natlex4.detail?p_isn=100429&p_lang=en.
Kearney. (n.d.). *Locations*. https://www.kearney.com/locations.
Keo, P. T., & Jun, A. (2016). Higher education institutions and ASEAN: Current trends and implications for future innovation and change. In C. S. Collins, M. N. Lee, J. N. Hawkins, & D. E. Neubauer (Eds.), *The Palgrave Handbook of Asia Pacific Higher Education* (pp. 615–624). Palgrave Macmillan.
Kim, A., Ryu, S., Kim, S., & Lepak, D. P. (2017). Determinants of the strategic involvement of human resource departments: Evidence from large South Korean firms. *Asia Pacific Journal of Human Resources, 55*, 44–63. https://doi.org/10.1111/1744-7941.12131.
Kuroda, K. (2016). Regionalization of higher education in Asia. In C. S. Collins, M. N. Lee, J. N. Hawkins, & D. E. Neubauer (Eds.), *The Palgrave handbook of Asia Pacific higher education* (pp. 113–127). Palgrave Macmillan.
Lee, S.-H. (2008). A theoretical framework on the role of HRM practices in family business succession. In P. H. Phan & J. E. Butler (Eds.), *Theoretical developments and future research in family business* (pp. 261–286). Information Age Publishing Inc.
Lim, L. Y., & Pang, E. F. (1982). Vertical linkages and multinational enterprises in developing countries. *World Development, 10*(7), 585–595.
Lin, D. (2017). *Bringing Industry 4.0 to life for companies in Southeast Asia*. Mckinsey & Company. https://www.mckinsey.com/~/media/McKinsey/Locations/Asia/Singapore/Our%20insights/DCC%20Singapore/DCC%20Singapore.pdf.
Marquardt, M., & Engel, D. (1993). *Global human resource development*. Prentice Hall.
McKinsey & Company. (n.d.). *Our offices*. https://www.mckinsey.com/locations.
McLean, G. N., & Akaraborworn, C. T. (2015). HRD education in developing countries. *Advances in Developing Human Resources, 17*(2), 213–238. https://doi.org/10.1177/1523422315572622.
McLean, G. N. (2021). "To reach the unreachable star" (The man of la Mancha) by making Vietnam's HRD impossible dream possible. In H. T. Tran, T. T. Phuong, H. T. M. Van, G. N. McLean, & M. A. Ashwill (Eds.), *Human resource development in Vietnam: Research and practice* (pp. 325–351). Palgrave Macmillan.
Menkhoff, T., & Labig, C. E. (1996). Trading networks of Chinese entrepreneurs in Singapore. *Sojourn, 11*(1), 128–151.

National Institute of Standards and Technology. (n.d.). *Core values and concepts*. https://www.nist.gov/baldrige/core-values-and-concepts.

OECD. (2019). Economic outlook for Southeast Asia, China and India 2020: Rethinking education for the digital era. *OECD Publishing*. https://doi.org/10.1787/1ba6cde0-en.

Park, S. H., Ungson, G. R., & Francisco, J. P. S. (2017). *ASEAN champions: Emerging stalwarts in regional integration*. Cambridge University Press.

Petrosea. (2019). *Bertransformasi: Untuk Massa Depan Yang Berkelanjutan* [Transforming for a sustainable future]. https://www.petrosea.com/wp-content/uploads/2020/04/PTRO_Annual_Report-2019__-.pdf.

Phuong, T. T., Duong, H. B., & McLean, G. N. (2015). Faculty development in Southeast Asian higher education: A review of the literature. *Asia Pacific Education Review, 16*, 107–117. https://doi.org/10.1007/s12564-015-9353-1

Pitiyanuwat, S. (2011). Education in South-East Asia: Quality assurance in South-East Asian higher education. In C. Brock & L. P. Symaco (Eds.), *Education in South-East Asia* (pp. 305–322). Symposium Books.

Prospects. (n.d.). *About us*. https://www.prospectsasean.com/about/.

Quang, T. T., Pimpa, N., & Burgess, J. (2020). Skill development: Vocational education institutions and industry engagement in the garment and textile industy. *Humanities & Social Sciences Reviews, 8*(4), 561–568. https://doi.org/10.18510/hssr.2020.8455.

QS Top Universities. (2021). *QS world university rankings*. https://www.topuniversities.com/university-rankings/world-university-rankings/2021.

Ra, S., Shrestha, U., Khatiwada, S., Yoon, S. W., & Kwon, K. (2019). The rise of technology and impact on skills. *International Journal of Training Research, 17*(1), 26–40. https://doi.org/10.1080/14480220.2019.1629727.

Regional Association of Vocational and Technical Education in Asia. (n.d.). *RAVTE activities*. http://www.ravte-asia.rmutt.ac.th/document/.

Schröder, T. (2019). A regional approach for the development of TVET systems in the light of the 4th industrial revolution: The regional association of vocational and technical education in Asia. *International Jouranl of Training Research, 17*(1), 83–95. https://doi.org/10.1080/14480220.2019.1629728.

Sembcorp Marine. (2019). *Embracing challenges & opportunities in a changing landscape: Sustainability report 2019*. https://www.sembmarine.com/scm2016/wp-content/uploads/2020/03/Sembcorp-Marine-SR2019.pdf.

ShanghaiRanking. (2020). *Academic ranking of world universities*. http://www.shanghairanking.com/ARWU2020.html.

Singapore-Myanmar Vocational Training Institute. (n.d.). *Events & News*. https://www.smvti-mm.org/events-news.

SkillsFuture. (n.d.). *About SkillsFuture*. https://www.skillsfuture.gov.sg/AboutSkillsFuture.

SkillsFuture. (2021). *Frequently asked questions*. https://www.myskillsfuture.gov.sg/content/portal/en/header/faqs/skillsfuture-credit.html.

Society for Human Resource Management. (n.d.). *Home*. https://www.shrm.org/pages/default.aspx.

Sugimura, M. (2012). The function of regional networks in East Asian higher education. In J. N. Hawkins, K. H. Mok, & D. E. Neubauer (Eds.), *Higher education regionalization in Asia Pacific: Implications for governance, citizenship, and university transformation* (pp. 45–64). Palgrave Macmillan.

Sustainable Agriculture & Environment Development Association. (n.d.). *About SAEDA*. http://saeda.net.

Symaco, L. P., & Tee, M. Y. (2019). Social responsibility and engagement in higher education: Case of the ASEAN. *International Journal of Educational Development, 66*, 18–192. https://doi.org/10.1016/j.ijedudev.2018.10.001.

Theingi, Purchase, S., & Phungphol, Y. (2008). Social capital in Southeast Asian business relationships. *Industrial Marketing Management, 37*(5), 523–530. https://doi.org/10.1016/j.indmarman.2007.09.014.

Tilak, J. B. (2003). Vocational education and training in Asia. In J. P. Reeves & R. Watanabe (Eds.), *International handbook of educational research in the Asia-Pacific Region* (pp. 673–686). Springer.

Times Higher Education. (2021). *World University Rankings 2021*. https://www.timeshighereducation.com/world-university-rankings/2021/world-ranking#!/page/0/length/25/sort_by/rank/sort_order/asc/cols/stats.

Triono, M. B., & Moses, K. M. (2019). Technical and vocational education and training and training in Indonesia. In B. Bai & Paryono (eds.), *Vocational education and training in ASEAN member states: Current status and future development* (pp. 45–80). Springer.

Umemiya, N. (2008). Regional quality assurance activity in higher education in Southeast Asia: Its characteristics and driving forces. *Quality in Higher Education, 14*(3), 277–290. https://doi.org/10.1080/13538320802507679.

U.S. News & World Report. (2021). *Best global universities*. https://www.usnews.com/education/best-global-universities.

World Bank. (2013). *ASEAN integration monitoring report*. https://openknowledge.worldbank.org/bitstream/handle/10986/16695/83914pdf.pdf?sequence=1&isAllowed=y.

Yeoh, B. S. A., & Huang, S. (2018). Family, migration and the gender politics of care. In A. McGregor, L. Law, & F. Miller (Eds.), *Routledge handbook of Southeast Asian development* (pp. 173–185). Routledge.

Yoto. (2016). Vocational education development strategy to improve the quality of human resources in dealing with ASEAN Economic Community.

AIP Conference Proceedings, 1778(030047). https://doi.org/10.1063/1.4965781.

Yusef, A. A., Santoso, H., Kojima, M., & Anas, T. (2019). *Human resources development in Indonesia—towards 2045.* https://www.eria.org/uploads/media/ERIA_PB_FY2019_06.pdf.

Zakaria, Z., & Halim, M. A. S. A. (2016). The mediating effect of family support in influencing business competitiveness of SME. In Sidek, N. Z. M. & Ismail S. M. (eds.), *Proceedings of the ASEAN entrepreneurship conference 2014* (pp. 29–37). Springer.

Zobrist, B., & McCormick, P. (2017). Primary and secondary education in Myanmar: Challenges facing current reforms. In L. H. Guan (ed.), *Education and globalization in Southeast Asia* (pp. 166–194). ISEAS—Yusof Ishak Institute.

CHAPTER 5

Individuals and Organizations: The Micro Dimension

The third dimension of the Regional HRD ecosystem in Southeast Asia is the micro dimension, which includes both contract workers and employees as well as organizations. These primary actors and facilitators of HRD engage in a "traditional dyad or two-party relationship that is central to employment and work" (Garavan et al., 2019, p. 268). In this context, primacy is placed on workers and employees as recipients of HRD interventions and organizations as direct facilitators of HRD in the exchange. Thus, this dimension is informed by social exchange theory (Blau, 1964) and social learning theory (Bandura, 1977, 1986), both of which demonstrate the essential role that dyadic interactions play for learning and development.

Research has shown how dyadic relationships between employees, workers, and organizations shape HRD on the individual and organizational levels, which form a crucial component of Regional HRD in Southeast Asia and ASEAN. The more integrated the organizations are in the regional economy, the more they influence Regional HRD policy and practice. However, given that the vast majority of organizations in Southeast Asia are small- and medium-sized enterprises (SMEs), non-governmental organizations (NGOs), and community-based organizations (CBOs), they have a substantial impact on the ecosystem at large. Existing research shedding light on the micro dimension of Regional

O. S. Crocco, *Developing Human Resources in Southeast Asia*, Palgrave Macmillan Asian Business Series,
https://doi.org/10.1007/978-3-030-79697-6_5

HRD in Southeast Asia includes studies on employee engagement and organizational citizenship behaviors in Thai organizations (Rurkkhum & Bartlett, 2012), leadership development programs in the Philippines (Rhea, 2013), and organizational support and work-life experiences in Malaysian organizations (Au & Ahmed, 2015). This chapter describes this micro dimension, discusses the role of individual workers and employees, and provides examples of organizations that exemplify a variety of HRD foci.

5.1 Employees and Workers

5.1.1 Central actors

The end goal of Regional HRD is the development of individuals in the workforce who then contribute to regional development and growth as a whole. From this perspective, employees and workers comprise the "central actor[s]" (Garavan et al., 2019, p. 268) in the Regional HRD ecosystem. There is intentionality behind the linguistic decision to speak about workers and not just employees. Specifically, there is a growing prevalence of contract workers who, although maybe not considered employees, are still invested in developing themselves (or being developed by those who hire them) to better perform their work. Limiting the discussion to employees would leave out, for example, the nearly 3 million contracted workers of Grab, the Singaporean-based ride-hailing company with operations in many Southeast Asian countries (Ezzatul et al., 2019). Still, despite this growing population, the vast majority of the literature focuses on employees of traditional organizations (Garavan et al., 2019).

Both employees and workers are a vital component of the Regional HRD ecosystem in Southeast Asia because they are the direct recipients of organizational or governmental efforts to facilitate HRD. It is the skills, knowledge, mindsets, and experience of employees and workers that are cultivated. As actors, however, employees and workers are also responsible for their own development. As much as we talk about the role of organizations, countries, and the region as a whole in developing human resources, it is ultimately up to individuals, if they so choose, to pursue learning and develop themselves to the best of their abilities given the current context. The key agent or actor of HRD is always the individual. Even though McLean and McLean (2001) define HRD as being to "the benefit of an organization, community, nation, or ultimately, the whole of humanity," they recognize that the mechanism through which this occurs is the development of individual adults in the workforce. Not only are employees and workers the recipients of HRD efforts, but they are also ultimately the actors that drive change, firm growth, and national and regional development. Herein we see, yet again, the inextricable connection and interaction between the dimensions of the Regional HRD ecosystem.

As a region, Southeast Asia boasts fairly low unemployment rates, with the highest rates found in Lao PDR at 9.1% and Brunei at 8.7% in 2018. The unemployment rate can sometimes be a fickle data point for considering the status of a workforce. For example, whereas Myanmar struggles in many other areas economically, its reported unemployment rate in 2018 was 0.9% (ASEAN, 2020). Similarly, Cambodia's in 2017 was 0.1% (ASEAN, 2020). When surveying employment by occupation (see Table 5.1), we see a divide between countries with a large share of their workforce engaged in professional and technical occupations, e.g., Singapore (42.9%), Brunei (30.9%), and Malaysia (22.9%), and countries with a large proportion engaged in agricultural, animal husbandry, forestry, fishing, and hunting occupations, e.g., Cambodia (42.5%), Lao PDR (42.2%),

Table 5.1 Proportion of employment by occupation

Country	*Professional, technical, and related*	*Administrative, executive, and managerial*	*Clerical and related*	*Services and sales*	*Agriculture, husbandry, forestry*	*Production and related*	*Other*
Brunei	30.9	7.7	10.1	20.2	0.7	14.6	15.8
Cambodia	3.5	0.8	2.5	16.3	42.5	17.7	16.7
Indonesia	7.6	1.5	6.0	25.5	36.6	31.1	1.8
Lao PDR	8.4	11.5	2.0	10.9	42.2	16.7	8.2
Malaysia	22.9	4.6	8.4	22.6	6.2	22.8	12.4
Myanmar	4.6	0.5	1.7	17.8	38.5	17.7	19.2
Philippines	9.7	11.4	6.1	18.4	11.8	15.6	27.0
Singapore	42.9	15.4	10.5	11.7	0.0	9.9	9.6
Thailand	5.6	3.7	4.5	20.1	28.8	21.2	16.1
Vietnam	11.6	1.0	2.0	17.5	7.5	25.8	34.7
Average	14.77	5.81	5.38	18.1	21.48	19.31	16.15

Note All data is for the year 2019 except Cambodia (2012), Lao PDR (2017), and Myanmar (2018); No data for Timor-Leste was available
Source ASEAN (2020)

Myanmar (38.5%), Indonesia, (36.3%), and Thailand (28.8%) (ASEAN, 2020). This divide has the potential to influence how and for whom HRD is prioritized across Southeast Asian countries.

5.1.2 *Value of HRD for Individuals*

The value of HRD for workers and employees is first and foremost intrinsic, as it leads to their enrichment and growth (Kuchinke, 2010). HRD is directly related to human development (Sen, 1999) and human capabilities development (Nussbaum, 2011), in that it is the primary mechanism that individuals can use for themselves or that organizations and governments can support for individuals. The relation of HRD to human development generally is why Aubrey (2020) and the ASEAN Human Development Organization have sought to reframe HRD or HRM as human development.

HRD for individuals is also valuable at the regional level, as shown by the research on the ASEAN Economic Community (AEC) mentioned in previous chapters. For ASEAN and the AEC to be successful, employees and workers need to have opportunities to develop themselves. This need was elucidated clearly in the context of Thailand, where communication and technical skill development were found to be instrumental in its workforce struggles when compared to its Southeast Asian neighbors (Nguyen, 2015). Similarly, in Cambodia, both the public and private sectors participate in developing the human resources of workers and employees as a means of preparing the workforce for the AEC (Rana & Ardichvili, 2014). As a whole, developing human resources is critical for Southeast Asia to reach "institutionalised regionalism," where the institutions of the region are strengthened to a point where regionalization goals, like those outlined in the ASEAN Charter, can be realized (Rattanasevee, 2014).

HRD also has immense business value as it relates to the cultivation of an organization's intellectual capital, which includes "the commitment and competence of workers" (Ulrich, 1998, p. 15). In a study of intellectual capital in the banking sector in Indonesia, Lao PDR, the Philippines, Thailand, and Vietnam, Rochmadhona et al. (2018) found that intellectual capital at the level of employees positively affects financial performance and competitive advantage. In Indonesia, micro, small, and medium enterprises ranked human resources as the top priority for developing their organizations against a variety of other priorities such as innovation, marketing, reputation development, and operations

(Ristyawan, 2020). A study of the relationship between learning and transfer of training in Malaysia found, not only that this relationship was strong, but also that focusing on knowledge and skill development during training had the potential for the greatest impact on the organization (Zumrah, 2013). Similarly, in small enterprises in Malaysia, management practices, in particular training, were a significant predictor of firm success (Yaacob et al., 2016). Clearly, there is immense value for organizations of all kinds to support the development of individual workers and employees, which is why HRD is such a high priority.

5.1.3 Formal Training

Given the importance of private enterprise for economic growth broadly, and the role that individual workers and employees play in firm success, it can be helpful to look at data on workers and employees in private firms in the region. Enterprise Surveys provide a representative sample of a country's firms, classified as small (5–9 employees), medium (10–99 employees), and large (100+ employees). This data has been used in a variety of ways in the region, such as predicting the role of foreign ownership, R&D, and innovation in ASEAN member countries (Nguyen-Van & Chang, 2019), but also offers details about workers and training (see Table 5.2). Based on this data, we see that the vast majority of workers in Southeast Asian firms are permanent workers; only a small percentage are temporary. Firms in Timor-Leste and Vietnam are the exceptions to this trend with over 10% of workers serving in temporary roles, nearly double the global and Southeast Asian averages.

Firms in Thailand lead the way in terms of offering training to the largest percentage of workers at 94%, well above the Southeast Asian and global averages of 61 and 49%, respectively. This finding must be tempered by the percentage of Thai firms offering formal training at all (see Table 5.2), which is only 18%. Workers in the Philippines are the biggest recipients of formal training because nearly 60% of the firms offer formal training and the proportion of workers offered training at those firms is 75%. On the other end of the spectrum would be Timor-Leste and Indonesia, in which only 1.9 and 7.2% of firms offer formal training, respectively. Furthermore, only 49% of the workers at the Indonesian firms are provided with training. When compared to the global average of 49%, the percentage of employees offered training by Southeast Asian firms on average, 61%, is competitive. Where Southeast Asian firms are

Table 5.2 HRD of employees and workers in Southeast Asia

Country	*Number of workers*	*Proportion of permanent workers (out of all workers)*	*Proportion of temporary workers (out of all workers)*	*Proportion of workers offered formal training (%)*
Cambodia	26.8	98.5	1.5	–
Indonesia	21.6	98.2	1.8	48.5
Lao PDR	17.9	98.1	1.9	49.8
Malaysia	32.5	97.2	2.8	33.4
Myanmar	25.1	99.2	0.8	57.7
Philippines	37.7	92.1	7.9	75.3
Thailand	44.7	100	0	93.7
Timor-Leste	25.4	89.5	10.5	–
Vietnam	52.5	85.5	14.5	65.6[a]
Southeast Asia	31.5	95.4	4.6	60.6
East Asia and the Pacific	43.2	95.3	4.7	66
Global	35.3	94.8	5.2	49.4

Note Cambodia: 373 firms; 64 Large (100+); 116 Medium (20–99); 193 Small (5–9); latest data from 2016
Indonesia: 1320 firms; 386 Large (100+); 452 Medium (20–99); 482 Small (5–9); latest data from 2015; Lao PDR: 332 firms; 22 Large (100+); 72 Medium (20–99); 238 Small (5–9); latest data from 2018; Malaysia: 1000 firms; 314 Large (100+); 343 Medium (20–99); 343 Small (5–9); latest data from 2015; Myanmar: 607 firms; 84 Large (100+); 161 Medium (20–99); 362 Small (5–9); latest data from 2016; Philippines: 1335 firms; 403 Large (100+); 514 Medium (20–99); 418 Small (5–9); latest data from 2015; Thailand: 1000 firms; 276 Large (100+); 324 Medium (20–99); 400 Small (5–9); latest data from 2016; Timor-Leste: 126 firms; 9 Large (100+); 34 Medium (20–99); 83 Small (5–9); latest data from 2015; Vietnam: 996 firms; 278 Large (100+); 383 Medium (20–99); 335 Small (5–9); latest data from 2015
[a] Denotes latest data available from 2009
Source World Bank (n.d.)

lagging behind is the percentage of firms offering formal training at all, which is a meager 20% compared to 32% globally and 34% in East Asia and the Pacific.

5.1.4 *Creativity and Innovation*

Organizations seek to cultivate creativity in their employees and workers as a means of gaining a competitive advantage. One study of over 700 SMEs in Southeast Asia found that human capital and an entrepreneurial orientation were needed for developing innovativeness (Ismail & Alam,).

In organizations, HRD plays a key role in developing human capital to bring about innovativeness. Developing innovativeness also has to do with the extent to which an organization invests in research and development (R&D). In a study of 1700 Southeast Asian firms, the human capital of a firm was a key predictor of whether that firm invested in R&D as a means to foster innovation (Zhang & Islam, 2020).

One form of training and learning design that has great potential for skill development, especially in light of the COVID-19 pandemic, is online and virtual learning. Effective online course design can enhance skills related to creativity and innovation in the Southeast Asian context (Somkram, 2017). These types of online courses have largely been under the purview of higher education institutions and large corporations, which use learning management systems and internal online training courses. Generally speaking, online training and development options, especially for those in small- and medium-sized enterprises, are limited. In a 2007 study of SMEs in Malaysia, Hooi found that only 43% of surveyed companies even offered information about training in online formats, much less offered the actual training online. In sectors such as healthcare, however, online training has been successful in cases such as the use of simulation-based training for healthcare providers in a low-resource intensive care unit (Emani et al., 2018).

There can also be opportunities for worker-to-worker development through processes such as mentoring. In a study of the role of line managers in facilitating HRD in Malaysian firms, mentoring proved to be an important way, other than continued professional development, to contribute to lifelong learning and the development of the employees (Ramachandra et al., 2011). We also know that, at the individual level, HRD affects an employee's commitment to an organization. In a study of Vietnamese pharmacists, those who perceived opportunities for career advancement and felt respected by their leaders had higher levels of organizational commitment (Dung et al., 2019). This commitment is another reason that HRD plays such an important part in the relationship between workers and employees and the organizations for which they work.

5.2 Organizations

A discussion of the micro dimension of Regional HRD would not be complete without addressing the role that organizations play in facilitating HRD for individuals. There are three key characteristics of organizations that influence the HRD ecosystem. They are the length of time it has existed in its location, its experience in delivering HRD, and the extent to which HRD policy and practice is strictly centralized around its strategic objectives (Garavan et al., 2019). From a regional perspective, the more broadly an organization is integrated into the Southeast Asian economy, the more its HRD practices and policies influence the region as a whole.

Park et al. (2017) have collected a group of emerging firms that they term "ASEAN Champions." These successful Southeast Asian-based firms not only possess "sustained success, prominence, and visibility in their respective local markets" but also are emerging as major regional players (Park et al., 2017, p. 4). It is worth considering how organizations like the firms mentioned by Park et al. (2017) use policy and practice to facilitate HRD in a way that is integrated into the region as a whole. Although none of these organizations are exemplars in all aspects of their operations, they have each set an agenda that centralizes HRD as a mechanism for achieving a competitive advantage. Many of the practices and policies laid out here are not unique to firms in Southeast Asia; however, they provide cogent examples of the value placed on HRD by major organizations in the region.

Bangkok Cable Co. Ltd, a manufacturing firm of electrical wires and cables in Thailand, has a long history of investing in the development of its human resources (Rogovsky & Tolentino, 2010). The company has an internal certification program that awards participants who complete their in-house training, the latter of which includes structured time for workers to share the learning and experience they have gained either inside or outside of the company (Rogovsky & Tolentino, 2010). This strategy frames their training as both an act of individual development and one inextricably tied to the collective success of the firm. The focus on developing its human resources is connected not only to the firm's financial success but also to its sustainable growth (Bangkok Cable, n.d.). Another Thai company, the automotive dealer and distributor S. P. International Co., includes "human resource development" in their organizational philosophy (S. P. International, n.d.) and connects it to their success. They employ several key HRD initiatives such as professional training for executives and ongoing training courses on emerging technology for their technicians (Rogovsky & Tolentino, 2010).

Indonesia's PT Petrosea Tbk., which specializes in mining, infrastructure, and oil and gas, is another exemplar in terms of developing its human resources, including employees at its six subsidiaries. The organization has a culture that values learning and development and, as a result, offers a variety of employee development and technical training programs (PT Petrosea Tbk., n.d.). To help execute these various HRD-related endeavors, the organization has its own Petrosea Academy and a "Human Capital and Organization Development" department (Park et al., 2017, p. 175).

In Singapore, the marine engineering company Sembcorp Marine Ltd., which operates shipyards in both Singapore and Indonesia, describes its culture as "people-centric," where employees can "enjoy their work and realise their potential" (Sembcorp Marine, n.d., p. 3). In its 2019 Sustainability Report, the organization outlines its human capital strategy in five areas, three of which are directly related to HRD: (a) "talent planning & leadership development," (b) "workforce capability & competency development," and (c) "employee engagement & well-being" (Sembcorp Marine, 2019, p. 36). Recent activities in these areas include a Global Leadership Development Program in collaboration with Singapore Management University. This mentorship program pairs new employees with more experienced employees, and provides sophisticated augmented reality and virtual reality training programs for their technicians (Sembcorp Marine, 2019). This serves as yet another example of the ecosystem having interconnected and mutually supporting actors, in this case higher education institutions.

Holcim Philippines is part of a Swiss-based multinational, which merged with French company Lafarge in 2015 to create LafargeHolcim. Holcim Philippines is a cement supplier with offices all over the Philippines and headquarters in Taguig City, just southeast of Manila. The organization touts a "people development thrust" to "boost high performance culture" (Holcim Philippines, 2019, p. 17). Part of this thrust is a focus on its Career Development Program, "which provides career opportunities for employees who wish to deepen their level of expertise in their chosen fields" (Holcim Philippines, 2019, p. 17). This program also serves as a mechanism for internal talent development and retention, which the company sees as vital to its success. Holcim Philippines has extended its HRD efforts beyond its employees into the community as well. In 2019, they worked alongside the government of the Philippines, specifically with the Technical Education and Skills Development Authority, to offer an industrial skills training course in a variety of subjects to a host community (Holcim Philippines, 2019). Here we see how HRD at the organizational level connects with HRD at the community level.

Jollibee Foods Corporation (JFC) is a multinational food corporation based in Pasig City in the Philippines. The organization sees its "family-oriented approach to personnel management" as the key to its enduring success in the Philippines and beyond (Jollibee, n.d., para 1). This approach, along with its focus on culturally relevant product offerings (e.g., "pineapples and rice") to differentiate itself from Western competitors (Vielmetter & Sell, 2014, p. 26), has made JFC successful in the Philippines and other Southeast Asian countries. The company also has a learning management system called the JFC Learning Web, where it offers easily accessible training courses and information to employees.

This focus on culture is also important to companies like the import–export firm Dao-Heuang Group, famous for its coffee in Lao PDR (Dao-Heuang Group, n.d.), which draws roughly 30% of its workforce from Thailand and Vietnam. Dao-Heuang utilizes leadership development programs for employees at all levels (not just executives or high potentials) as well as mentorship programs for emerging young leaders with senior leaders in the firm (Park et al., 2017). Given the number of non-Lao employees, Dao-Heuang's HRD efforts must take into consideration non-Lao cultural factors.

Phnom Penh Water Supply Authority (PPWSA) in Cambodia provides a good example of HRD in municipal organizations in Southeast Asia as well. PPWSA relies on ongoing training, both in-house and external, which even includes sending employees to other water utility companies to learn and then report back to the organization (Park et al., 2017). PPWSA has run its own training center since 1997. Concerning educational attainment, the largest segment of its employees, 27.92%, includes those with diplomas or short course training (PPWSA, n.d.). Given the low levels of higher education in Cambodia generally, the internal training processes are even more important for the sustained success of the organization.

Looking at the Enterprise Surveys data above, we see that, by and large, labor regulations are not a major constraint for Southeast Asian firms. Only 5.6% of firms identify regulations as a concern, which is nearly 50% less than the global average of 10.7% (see Table 5.3). This lack of concern is not surprising, considering that the ASEAN Way lacks an enforcement mechanism and leaves it up to the individual countries or firms themselves to opt into many of its qualification frameworks or not.

Table 5.3 HRD in organizations in Southeast Asia

Country	*Percent of firms offering formal training*	*Percent of firms identifying labor regulations as a major constraint*	*Percent of firms identifying an inadequately educated workforce as a major constraint*	*Proportion of skilled workers (out of all production workers) (%)*
Cambodia	22.2	5.2	17.6	80.2
Indonesia	7.2	9.9	10.8	82.8
Lao PDR	24.4	0.2	11.8	79.2
Malaysia	18.5	9.2	12.2	88.9
Myanmar	5.9	1.4	9.6	54.3
Philippines	59.8	3.5	10.1	82.8
Thailand	18	10.6	2.1	87.2
Timor-Leste	1.9	6.4	13.5	79.3
Vietnam	22.2	3.8	8.1	73.9
Southeast Asia	20.1	5.6	10.6	78.7
East Asia and the Pacific	34	6	12.2	77.6
Global	32.3	10.7	20.5	76.6

Note See note from Table 5.2
Source World Bank (n.d.)

Also not surprising is the fact that Cambodia and Timor-Leste lead the region in the percentage of their firms that identify the lack of an educated workforce as a major constraint to their success. Still, when compared to the global average of 20.5% of firms identifying this lack as a major constraint, it is encouraging that only 11% of Southeast Asian firms do. Lack of an educated workforce, however, increases the weight and impact of HRD on organizations, communities, and nations.

But not only so-called ASEAN Champions or large Southeast Asian organizations are developing human resources. Small community-based organizations, NGOs, and other SMEs also facilitate HRD, contributing to the greater Regional HRD ecosystem. Unfortunately, in places like Lao PDR where the vast majority of employers are SMEs, the latter do not have a strong interest in skill development and look to government, donors, or NGOs to support it (Phoumilay, 2019).

NGOs interface with businesses, national and local governments, development organizations, and other civil society organizations to perform a variety of functions. Capacity building, which includes training and fits broadly under HRD, is often a key focus area of NGOs (Turner, 2011). In the Philippines, NGOs participate in capacity building through skill development in local communities, typically poor and marginalized ones (Turner, 2011). In a study of tourism in three rural communities in Thailand, Malaysia, and Indonesia, "capacity development" was the single most important component of a community's ability to develop entrepreneurial skills and advance tourism services (Bouchon & Rawat, 2016, p. 50). Even libraries and NGOs associated with reading can support adult literacy rates and lifelong learning, as is the case in the community learning centers in Vietnam (Hossain, 2016).

One educational and training organization that we studied in Southeast Myanmar (Crocco & Cseh, 2021) illustrates how a CBO can influence HRD and thereby contribute to Regional HRD. Founded in 2005, this organization offers young people training in a variety of subjects such as the English language, civics, management, and leadership to prepare them for their next steps, whether into higher education or the workforce. In this case, the organization tries to compensate for the poor educational system and ill-prepared workforce in rural Myanmar. Many of the alumni of this program have gone on to found organizations and businesses of their own, both in the community and beyond. The leader of the organization was even able to provide training and further education for several staff members to develop their skills. In addition to formal training and learning programs, we found that social learning, e.g., learning through modeling based on social learning theory (Bandura, 1977), played a role in the learning and change processes of the organization (Crocco & Cseh, 2021). This case shows that CBOs can provide HRD for their staff members. But in addition, it shows that they can have an entire program that is itself HRD-related and further builds capacity in a community's young people, who can then influence many others in this and surrounding communities.

One important point of comparison between HRD programs and practices in large corporations and NGOs and CBOs is that the former have policy frameworks that construe HRD within a relatively centralized model. Thus, all of their endeavors are meant to develop their employees and workers to work more effectively within the corporation's strategic priorities. In this sense, HRD also serves as a mechanism for promoting retention. In contrast, NGOs and CBOs often offer HRD in the form of capacity building for their employees and communities at large, knowing full well (and even purposefully leading to the fact) that employees may use their new skills in a variety of ways, including leaving the organization entirely to pursue what they may view as equally meaningful work. While generally positive for those communities at large, this approach can also lead to redundancies or less efficient uses of HRD within a particular organization (Garavan et al., 2019).

Promoting HRD to support SMEs has long been a strategy in ASEAN, beginning with the 2004–2014 ASEAN Policy Blueprint for SME Development, which was later expanded upon in the 2016–2025 ASEAN Strategic Action Plan for SME Development (ASEAN, 2015). The relevance of the first blueprint for SMEs, particularly in the context of Cambodia, was articulated by Sotharith (2013). He wrote that the entrepreneurship development program "enhance[s] SME-sector skills in management and organization on a self-reliant basis," "foster[s] SME capabilities for inter-firm networking and linkages," and "track[s] and benchmarking SME capabilities, dynamism and competitiveness" (pp. 166–167). SME growth in Cambodia has increased dramatically over the last two decades. To support this growth, two Cambodian businessmen with support from the Cambodian government established the Federation of Associations of SME of Cambodia (FASMEC), an NGO that supports SME development. One aspect of FASMEC's mission is to provide "relevant vocational training and capacity building for SMEs" (Sotharith, 2013, p. 177).

Given that individuals are the primary actors in an HRD ecosystem and that organizations are the primary direct facilitators of HRD, the micro dimension of the Regional HRD ecosystem in Southeast Asia is the most dynamic and consequential. It is the most dynamic in that it is always changing and adjusting to market realities, organizational needs, and technological changes. It is also reactionary in response to national and regional economic and educational conditions, as we saw above with the cases of Cambodia and Myanmar. This juncture is where other actors such as international organizations come into play, as described in the previous chapter. Now that the three content dimensions of the Regional HRD ecosystem in Southeast Asia have been described, it is prudent to discuss the process dimensions of the ecosystem.

Bibliography

Association of Southeast Asian Nations. (2001). *Preparing workers for changes in the labour market: The ASEAN experience*. ASEAN Secretariat.

Association of Southeast Asian Nations. (2012). *ASEAN document series 2010*. The ASEAN Secretariat.

Association of Southeast Asian Nations. (2015). *ASEAN strategic action plan for SME development 2016–2025*. https://asean.org/wp-content/uploads/2015/12/SAP-SMED-Final.pdf.

Association of Southeast Asian Nations. (2020). *ASEAN statistical yearbook 2020*. https://www.aseanstats.org/wp-content/uploads/2020/12/ASYB_2020.pdf.

Au, W. C., & Ahmed, P. K. (2015). Exploring the effects of workplace support on work-life experience: A study of Malaysia. *Human Resource Development International, 18*(4), 346–365. https://doi.org/10.1080/13678868.2015.1019816.

Aubrey, R. (2020). *Leading human development in ASEAN: Using management concepts from ASEAN countries to create an authentic model of human development*. McGraw Hill.

Bandura, A. (1977). *Social learning theory*. Prentice-Hall, Inc.

Bandura, A. (1986). *Social foundations of thought and action: A social cognitive theory*. Prentice-Hall.

Bangkok Cable. (n.d.). *Sustainability*. https://www.bangkokcable.com/en/sustainability.

Blau, P. (1964). *Exchange and power in social life*. Wiley.

Bouchon, F., & Rawat, K. (2016). Rural areas of ASEAN and tourism services, a field for innovative solutions. *Procedia—Social and Behavioral Sciences, 224*, 44–51. https://doi.org/10.1016/j.sbspro.2016.05.398.

Crocco, O. S., & Bunwirat, N. (2014). English in ASEAN: Key effects. *International Journal of the Computer, the Internet and Management, 22*(2), 22–27.

Crocco, O. S., & Cseh, M. (2021). Learning, development, and change in a community-based enterprise in Myanmar. *European Journal of Training and Development, 45*(4/5), 436–448. https://doi.org/10.1108/EJTD-12-2019-0198.

Dao-Heuang Group. (n.d.). *About us*. https://www.daoheuanggroup.com/about.php.

Dung, L. T., Ho, D. P., Hiep, N. T. K., Hoi, P. T., & Hanh, D. T. P. (2019). Job satisfaction, leadership styles, demographic variables and organisational commitment among pharmacists in Vietnam. *The South East Asian Journal of Management, 13*(1), 37–52. https://doi.org/10.21002/seam.v13i1.10693.

Emani, S. S., Allan, C. K., Forster, T., Fisk, A. C., Lagrasta, C., Zheleva, B., Weinstock, P., & Thiagarajan, R. R. (2018). Simulation training improves team dynamics and performance in a low-resource cardiac intensive care unit. *Annals of Pediatric Cardiology, 11*(2), 130–136.

Ezzatul, A. D., Kee, D. M. H., Tuovi, H., Roslan, N. A. D. B., & Charlott, S. (2019). Case grab. *International Journal of Tourism & Hospitality in Asia Pacific, 2*(2), 1–12.

Garavan, T., McCarthy, A., & Carbery, R. (2019). An ecosystems perspective on international human resource development: A meta-synthesis of the literature. *Human Resource Development Review, 18*(2), 248–288. https://doi.org/10.1177/1534484319828865.

Holcim Philippines. (2019). *2019 Annual Report*. https://www.holcim.ph/sites/philippines/files/atoms/files/holcim_philippines_2019.pdf.

Hooi, L. A. (2007). Implementing e-HRM: The readiness of small and medium sized manufacturing companies in Malaysia. In C. Rowley & M. Warner (Eds.), *Management in South-East Asia* (pp. 74–94). Routledge.

Hossain, Z. (2016). Towards a lifelong learning society through reading promotion: Opportunities and challenges for libraries and community learning centres in Viet Nam. *International Review of Education, 62*(2), 205–219.

Ismail, M. D., & Alam, S. S. (2019). Innovativeness and competitive advantage among small and medium enterprise exporters: Evidence from emerging markets in South East Asia. *The South East Asian Journal of Management, 13*(1), 74–91. https://doi/org/https://doi.org/10.21002/seam.v13i1.9872.

Jollibee. (n.d.). *About us*. https://www.jollibee.com.ph/about-us/.

Kuchinke, K. P. (2010). Human development as a central goal for human resource development. *Human Resource Development International, 13*(5), 575–585.

McLean, G. N., & McLean, L. (2001). If we can't define HRD in one country, how can we define it in an international context? *Human Resource Development International, 4*(3), 313–326.

Nguyen, N. H. (2015). Thai workforce-ready for ASEAN Economic Community 2015? *UTCC International Journal of Business and Economics, 7*(1), 21–39.

Nguyen-Van, D., & Chang, C. (2019). Foreign ownership, R&D, and firm innovation in ASEAN countries: A generalized ordered logit model. *Management Dynamics in the Knowledge Economy, 7*(4), 521–534. https://doi.org/10.25019/MDKE/7.4.05.

Nussbaum, M. C. (2011). *Creating capabilities: The human development approach*. The Belknap Press of Harvard University Press.

Park, S. H., Ungson, G. R., & Francisco, J. P. S. (2017). *ASEAN champions: Emerging stalwarts in regional integration*. Cambridge University Press.

Phoumilay, P. (2019). Vocational education and training in Lao PDR. In B. Bai & Paryono (Eds.), *Vocational education and training in ASEAN member states: Current status and future development* (pp. 81–108). Springer.

Phnom Penh Water Supply Authority. (n.d.). *Human resource*. http://www.ppwsa.com.kh/en/index.php?page=human-resource.

PT Petreosea Ptk. (n.d.). *People*. https://www.petrosea.com/about-us/people/.

Ramachandra, A., Mansor, N. N. A., & Mohamed, A. (2011). Calling line managers in employee continuous professional development in South East Asia. *Intangible Capital, 7*(2), 356–374.

Rana, S., & Ardichvili, A. (2014). Cambodia and the ASEAN Economic Community: Opportunities, challenges, and implications for human resource development. *Reconsidering Development, 3*(1), 39–55.

Rattanasevee, P. (2014). Towards institutionalised regionalism: The role of institutions and prospects for institutionalisation in ASEAN. *Springerplus, 3*(556), 1–10. https://doi.org/10.1186/2193-1801-3-556.

Rhea, Z. M. (2013). Alien tutelage: On generalizability and contextualization in leadership development. *Human Resource Development International, 16*(3), 346–356. https://doi.org/10.1080/13678868.2012.756158.

Rochmadhona, B. N., Suganda, T. R., & Cahyadi, S. (2018). The competitive advantage between intellectual capital and financial performance of banking sector in ASEAN. *Jurnal Keuangan dan Perbankan, 22*(2), 321–334. https://doi.org/10.26905/jkdp.v22i2.2060.

Rogovsky, N., & Tolentino, A. (2010). *Sustainable enterprise promotion through good workplace practices and human resource management* (3rd ed.). International Training Centre of the International Labour Organization.

Rurkkhum, S., & Bartlett, K. R. (2012). The relationship between employee engagement and organizational citizenship behavior in Thailand. *Human Resource Development International, 15*(2), 157–174. https://doi.org/10.1080/13678868.2012.664693.

Sembcorp Marine. (n.d.). *Code of business conduct*. https://www.sembmarine.com/code-business-conduct.

Sembcorp Marine. (2019). *Embracing challenges & opportunities in a changing landscape: Sustainability Report 2019*. https://www.sembmarine.com/scm2016/wp-content/uploads/2020/03/Sembcorp-Marine-SR2019.pdf.

Sen, A. (1999). *Development as freedom*. Oxford University Press.

Somkram, N. (2017). Online course design for creativity and innovative skills in virtual cultural ASEAN community. *International Journal of Emerging Technologies in Learning, 12*(4), 4–20. https://doi.org/10.3991/ijet.v12i01.6032.

Sotharith, C. (2013). SME development in ASEAN: A Cambodian case study. In S. Basu Das (Ed.), *ASEAN economic community scorecard* (pp. 163–181). ISEAS——Yusof Ishak Institute.

Turner, M. (2011). How to win friends and influence people: Civic engagement in the Philippines. *Public Administration and Development, 31*, 91–101.

Ulrich, D. (1998). Intellectual capital = competence x commitment. *Sloan Management Review, 39*(2), 15–26.

Vielmetter, G., & Sell, Y. (2014). *Leadership 2030: The six megatrends you need to understand to lead your company into the future*. American Management Association.

World Bank. (n.d.). *Enterprise surveys*. https://www.enterprisesurveys.org/en/enterprisesurveys.

Yaacob, N. M., Mahmood, R., Zin, S. M., & Puteh, M. (2016). Factors affecting the performance of small business start-ups under Tunas Mekar programme. In N. Z. M. Sidek & S. M. Ismail (Eds.), *Proceedings of the ASEAN entrepreneurship conference 2014* (pp. 3–14). Springer.

Zhang, J., & Islam, M. S. (2020). The heterogeneous impacts of R&D on innovation in services sector: A firm-level study of developing ASEAN. *Sustainability, 12*(4), 1643. https://doi.org/10.3390/su12041643.

Zumrah, A. R. (2013). Is job satisfaction enhancing learning-training transfer relationship? *Journal of Workplace Learning, 25*(8), 543–555. https://doi.org/10.1108/JWL-02-2013-0005.

PART III

A Holistic Framework for the ASEAN Community

CHAPTER 6

Developing Human Resources the ASEAN Way

In addition to content dimensions, understanding an ecosystem like the one described in this book requires an investigation into the processes that occur within and among the content dimensions. In other words, if the content dimensions make up the *what, who*, and *where* of the Regional HRD ecosystem, then the process dimensions make up the *how* and *why*. How and why has the ecosystem emerged? How has it evolved? What mechanisms have allowed it to evolve? To describe all processes involved in this particular ecosystem is not feasible given its complexity; however, the goal of this chapter is to start unpacking the processes of the ecosystem's emergence, its convergence and divergence, and its continual adaptation and learning. By providing an overarching framework to allow readers to visualize this conceptualization of the ecosystem, the hope is that readers will begin to understand how the Regional HRD ecosystem is functioning and evolving.

6.1 Emergence

Understanding the process dimensions of an ecosystem begins with reflections on the emergence of the boundaries of the ecosystem. How did the ecosystem come to be? What key events can be shown as integral to the establishment of its boundaries? An HRD ecosystem emerges at the

O. S. Crocco, *Developing Human Resources in Southeast Asia*, Palgrave Macmillan Asian Business Series, https://doi.org/10.1007/978-3-030-79697-6_6

regional level as different actors—be they national governments, multinational corporations, non-governmental organizations (NGOs), individual workers themselves, or a regional organization—are bound together economically, socially, and politically in a way that the region's labor force becomes intertwined. In Southeast Asia, the regional organization of ASEAN has been a major contributor to the emergence of a Regional HRD ecosystem by contributing to the boundedness of the region. Even though ASEAN has kept Timor-Leste from full membership, ASEAN has done a great deal for the region in terms of demarcating its boundaries and building a regional identity. More directly related to HRD, ASEAN has laid out a vision, albeit disjointed at times, for developing human resources in the region. In doing so, ASEAN has put in place mechanisms to bring about HRD in the region. However, as is the case in other regions such as the EU (Kenny & Kinsella, 2015), neither a regional organization like AESAN nor any other single body controls the emergence of the HRD ecosystem. This lack of control is especially the case in the Southeast Asian context, given the role of cultural norms and institutions like the ASEAN Way, which is inherently averse to control, enforcement, and domination.

As a result of the diversity of countries represented in ASEAN and the legacy of colonialism in the region, the ASEAN Way emerged as a "process of interaction, socialization, compromise and adjustment" (Acharya, 1998, p. 57). The ASEAN Way influences policy and practice related to HRD in the region as national actors contribute and respond to this way of being. This interaction means that the vision of Regional HRD has evolved by consensus, through relationships, and, in general, slowly. Regional HRD has developed in such an unhurried fashion, that it has yet to fully coordinate its internal efforts, despite the idea of human resource development built into the fabric of ASEAN from its inception and reinforced in its constitution, the ASEAN Charter.

When we consider how the Regional HRD ecosystem emerged historically, it began in earnest when the region's countries began to group themselves as such. In this sense, even before ASEAN was founded in 1967, there existed regional organizations such as the Southeast Asian Ministers of Education Organization (SEAMEO), which was founded in 1965 with the initial member countries of Lao PDR, Malaysia, the Philippines, Singapore, Thailand, and Vietnam (SEAMEO, n.d.-a). While it was not until 1993 that it formed the Regional Centre for Higher Education, later the Regional Institution for Higher Education and Development

(RIHED), SEAMEO considered at length how to coordinate and collaborate on the region's educational development, an issue always relating to the development of a regional workforce (i.e., Regional HRD). Not only does SEAMEO predate ASEAN, but its membership includes Timor-Leste, which joined in 2006. In this sense, it has been nimbler and more adaptive as a regional organization than even ASEAN. SEAMEO and ASEAN hold their annual meetings at the same time to reduce travel demands for those involved, but they have remained separate organizations. To this day, SEAMEO-RIHED works on HRD-related projects such as the regional mobility of students (Hou et al.,) and technical and vocational training (TVET), teacher training, and higher education harmonization (SEAMEO, n.d.-b), all of which are related to HRD broadly. The pre-existence of SEAMEO illustrates that the emergence of this ecosystem did not rely exclusively on ASEAN, despite ASEAN being a major player. The relationship between SEAMEO and ASEAN is also an example of the boundaries of the ecosystem expanding over time. While efforts may have initially been focused on the realm of education, the boundaries have quickly expanded to all types of organizations and industries, both in the public and private sectors.

The most recent and compelling example of the emergence and expanding boundaries of the Regional HRD ecosystem in Southeast Asia is the new ASEAN Declaration on Human Resources Development for the Changing World of Work and Its Roadmap (ASEAN, 2020a) discussed in Chapter 3. This declaration is by far the most comprehensive vision for Regional HRD in Southeast Asia put forward. The roadmap describes the vision as "An ASEAN workforce that is future ready and equipped with competencies that enable them to actively and effectively contribute to the sustainable development, competitiveness and resilience of ASEAN" (ASEAN, 2020a, p. 7). In fact, the vision laid out here aligns fairly well with the preliminary definition of Regional HRD I and my colleague Oleksandr Tkachenko developed. We described Regional HRD as "A collective vision with corresponding activities for human resource development carried out by a group of countries for the benefit of their individuals, organizations, communities, nations, and the region as a whole" (Crocco & Tkachenko, 2020, p. 11). The roadmap attached to this ASEAN declaration outlines five desired outcomes with associated program areas for developing the region's human resources. These outcomes include (a) cultivating a lifelong learning culture; (b) improving inclusiveness in education and employment for everyone; (c) establishing competencies and qualifications in line with the demands and needs of the labor market; (d) increasing employability, employment opportunities, and job quality; and (e) developing "sound HRD policies and financing" (ASEAN, 2020a, p. 7). Under each desired outcome are specific actions with tentative timeframes, implementing bodies, and potential collaborators.

The vision and desired outcomes laid out in this document have expanded the boundaries and presence of the Regional HRD ecosystem more than any other single policy or practice. The fact that this expansion occurred under Vietnam's chairmanship is also exemplifies that emergence depends on the values and priorities of actors within the ecosystem (Garavan et al., 2019). The more a region, country, or organization prioritizes HRD, the more influential that entity will be on the ecosystem's evolution in that area. Given Vietnam's recent prioritization of HRD, it is not surprising that it has played such a significant role in facilitating Regional HRD.

6.2 Convergence and Divergence

In addition to the process of emergence, there are also processes of convergence and divergence within the Regional HRD ecosystem that have influenced its evolution. These processes are ongoing negotiations between actors in the ecosystem that clash, overlap, and supersede one another in terms of HRD systems, policies, and practices (Rawley & Benson, 2002). Considering the region's political, economic, and cultural diversity as outlined in Chapters 1 and 3, there is a large amount of convergence and divergence related to HRD.

Convergence and divergence can be used to understand the similar or contrasting experiences of actors across any number of dimensions and levels. In the Southeast Asian context, it is most helpful to look across four levels of analysis: national, subregional, regional, and global (Warner and Rowley (2007). Convergence and divergence happen within individual countries through national HRD-related programs such as TVET and at the subregional level through multi-country HRD projects, such as those found in the Initiative for ASEAN Integration (IAI). At the regional level, these processes are facilitated through programs that include all 11 countries in the region, such as SEAMEO-RIHED. Finally, at the global level, convergence and divergence occur through HRD-related efforts that extend beyond the region and include ASEAN dialogue partners (e.g., Australia, South Korea). Scholars point out that in general there is "far more homogeneity and convergence" within Southeast Asia than ever before (Acharya, 2012, p. 4). This consensus fits the thesis that globalization, the Asian Financial crisis of 1997, and increased communication has led to convergence dominating divergence in international HRD (Bartlett et al., 2002). However, it should be kept in mind that a lot of convergence in the Asian context generally has been considered "soft convergence," meaning that given the complexity and diversity of the region, there is less rigid convergence in the area of HRD and management practices broadly (Budhwar & Debrah, 2009, p. 203).

Regional partnerships in which countries can collaborate on HRD efforts will be vital to the success of an integrated Regional HRD ecosystem. For example, consider efforts at developing the competency of midwives in Lao PDR. Given Thailand's expertise in this area, the Thailand International Cooperation Agency worked with the Lao PDR Ministry of Health and the United Nations Population Fund to create training for midwifery educators across Lao PDR (Srisaeng & Upvall, 2020). This effort is a good example of convergence occurring in a variety of interconnected mechanisms in the Regional HRD ecosystem, including national governments, international organizations, higher education institutions, and workers and employees. While midwifery itself is not HRD in the traditional sense, this example highlights the convergence of training processes to facilitate development. Another example would be quality assurance (QA) in higher education. Individual countries have established their own QA measures while being informed by, and simultaneously informing, regional mechanisms for QA (Umemiya,). These QA mechanisms are not only being established within the region but are also being influenced by extra-regional organizations such as the Asia-Pacific Quality Network (Hou et al., 2015).

Efforts toward convergence in Regional HRD have also been made as the result of the ASEAN Economic Community and the desire for a single market and production base as well as the mostly free flow of skilled labor. Mutual recognition arrangements (MRAs), discussed in previous chapters, are illustrative of attempts to converge systems related to HRD in the region. As ASEAN member countries agree on the competencies of certain skilled labor areas (e.g., dentistry, accounting), they converge on the training and education required. Tourism and hospitality have also moved toward policy convergence in the sense that international standards are becoming more commonplace throughout Southeast Asia. The hospitality industry has experienced increased workforce mobility as a result of ASEAN and its MRAs for skilled labor. In terms of convergence regionally, tourism provides a good example by including HRD in the MRA for tourism professionals (ASEAN, 2018). Building on the work of the ASEAN Framework Agreement on Services signed in 1995 and the ASEAN Vision 2020 on Partnership in Dynamic Development signed in 1997, the focus on tourism mutual recognition emerged in 2002 with the signing of the ASEAN Tourism Agreement (ATA). This agreement included the agreement that "Member States shall cooperate in developing human resources in the tourism and travel industry" (ASEAN, 2018, p. 70). Not only that, but a key objective of the ATA was:

> to enhance mutual assistance in human resource development and strengthen cooperation to develop, upgrade and expand tourism and travel facilities and services in ASEAN and to create favourable conditions for the public and private sectors to engaged more deeply in tourism development, intra-ASEAN travel and investment in tourism services and facilities. (ASEAN, 2018, p. 72)

For example, HRD has played an explicit role in the emergence of Vietnam's Phu Quoc Island as a major tourist destination as a result of its attempt to become the next Bali or Phuket in the region (Pham & Thirumaran, 2016). Regionally, the Greater Mekong Subregion has been an area in which coordinated tourism efforts have relied on HRD. In particular, the Development Triangle Area, which includes 10 provinces in Vietnam, Cambodia, and Lao PDR, has been a focal area for governments to support cross-border tourism in the area by investing in HRD (Gam, 2021).

There has also been a lot of energy focused on sustainable tourism in Southeast Asia. From my time at Payap University, the growth of interest in ecotourism in the region has inspired initiatives such as a Center of Social Impact that leads sustainable tourism programs (Payap University, n.d.). This move toward sustainable ecotourism in the region is an embodiment of developing human resources the ASEAN Way. For example, the previous King of Thailand, HRM Bhumibol Adulyadej, was an advocate of what he termed the "Sufficiency Economy Philosophy," a vision for Thailand's development that has influenced the region's thinking as well. In this philosophy, King Bhumibol advocated for an orientation toward development challenges that focused on "the middle path" and "moderation," combining "patience, perseverance, diligence, wisdom, and prudence" (Mongsawad, 2010, p. 127). While human well-being and HRD are a key component of this philosophy, it is also related to the human relationship with the environment. In many ways, King Bhumibol's philosophical approach here resembles the ASEAN Way. Often frustratingly slow-moving to those outside of the region, convergence (and change in general) is slow, deliberate, adaptive, and relationship oriented. While not without its faults, the key benefit of the ASEAN Way is that it allows convergence to occur in a way that facilitates stakeholder buy-in.

The majority of this section has focused on convergence, which is one reason that Regional HRD is emerging and evolving. Convergence around HRD-related areas such as training is also one reason why Regional HRD is so intriguing. However, the extent and impact of convergence is easy to overestimate and overstate (Rowley, 2017). Divergence remains an important process in the ecosystem and is still prevalent in HRD systems, policies, and practices. Divergence can occur due to national culture and the influence of differences in cultural value dimensions on HRD practice. Even though there is convergence at the policy level and espoused convergence at the level of practice, there still may be notable divergence when it comes to practice or varying levels of acceptance of new ways of operating (Rowley & Benson, 2002). Similarly, even though there is convergence at the regional level, divergence can occur during implementation at the national level due to limited country resources.

Continuing with the above example of tourism professionals and tourism services in the region, while there have been attempts at policy and practice convergence, there has also been divergence due to regional disparities among countries and even within countries between urban and rural areas. While there are many cases of innovative HRD related to tourism in rural areas, there are still major gaps in resources and capacity building efforts in rural areas when compared to urban areas throughout Southeast Asia (Bouchon & Rawat, 2016). The significance of this disparity cannot be understated, especially given the fact that over half of Southeast Asian citizens live in rural areas (ASEAN, 2020b). Tourism is important because travel has been the largest intra-ASEAN export and intra-ASEAN import over the last ten years, representing over 43% of intra-ASEAN exports in services and 35% of intra-ASEAN imports in 2019 (ASEAN, 2020b). In 2019 alone, over 143 million visitors from around the world landed in ASEAN member countries, over a third of whom were citizens of other ASEAN member countries (ASEAN, 2020b).

One obvious attempt at convergence that relates to Regional HRD regards language. ASEAN established English as its only official language back in 2007 in an attempt to unify the region and provide a medium of communication (Crocco & Bunwirat, 2014). Thus, all of the training materials and the vast majority of HRD programs offered throughout the region are conducted in English. But at least in areas such as health worker mobility, divergence in language and qualifications can influence the quality of care (Te et al., 2018).

6.3 Continuous Adaptation and Learning

Another process within the Regional HRD ecosystem in Southeast Asia is that of continuous adaptation and learning. This ecosystem is continually evolving due to the feedback it receives from its constituents, which, in turn, influences future components of the system (Garavan et al., 2019). Forces of globalization; relations with external partners such as China, Japan, and the United States; and emerging civil society also influence regional identity in Southeast Asia (Acharya, 2012) and, therefore, affect the continual adaptation of the Regional HRD ecosystem.

I intentionally use the word "learning" here to emphasize that it is not a passive process of evolving but an active process in which actors (individuals, organizations, and governments) intentionally seek out opportunities to learn from others in the region. One way that actors are in a continuous process of adaptation and learning is through feedback loops that emerge in organizations across different levels of the ecosystem (Garavan et al., 2019). As mentioned in previous chapters, these processes can occur informally in mentoring and peer networks but also through organized conferences and forums where organizations and individuals can share best practices. While not a comprehensive list, conferences and forums in this area have included the Human Resource Management and Professional Development in the Digital Age conference, hosted in Singapore, and the ASEAN Human Resource Conference. In addition, the Academy of Human Resource Development has held its Asian conference in Thailand in 2018, Vietnam in 2019, and Malaysia in 2021. Given the global hub cities in the region such as Bangkok, Singapore, Jakarta,

Kuala Lumpur, and Manila, among others, Southeast Asia continues to host large international conferences related to HRD. Even organizations like Human Resources Online host regional conferences in the area that facilitate this continual adaptation and learning around HRD. In 2021 alone, Human Resources Online is hosting regional conferences on workforce mobility, learning and development, and HR technology (Human Resources Online, n.d.).

The phenomenon of outsourcing in Southeast Asia provides an interesting lens through which to view the importance of continuous adaptation and learning related to Regional HRD. As countries and organizations in the region participate in outsourcing, either as sending or receiving nations, it is an area where actors are constantly learning and adapting. Outsourcing occurs when organizations contract work out to third-party individuals or organizations. Offshore outsourcing occurs at a higher level when entire business operations are moved to a different country, typically from a more expensive to a less expensive nation where the organization can take advantage of lower labor and/or production costs. In Southeast Asia, the biggest offshore outsourcing player has been the Philippines. As a result of many years of partnership, and even temporary colonization from the United States, people in the Philippines are familiar with the English language but also many of the cultural aspects of delivering services to Americans. Many Filipinos are also trained in U.S. accounting services (Thangavelu & Chongvilaivan, 2013).

Thangavelu and Chongvilaivan (2013) identify four characteristics for work that can be outsourced, namely, it does not require face-to-face interaction, is labor-intensive, can be systematized and standardized, and can use technology such as the Internet and phone. With the emergence of 5G, the low cost of labor in Southeast Asia, and its workforce's increasing competence in the English language and cross-cultural communication, Southeast Asian countries are primed to be hubs for outsourcing. The top policy issue for outsourcing for ASEAN, according to Thangavelu and Chongvilaivan (2013), is skill development. They write, "workforce skills need to be continually upgraded, and the education systems improved" (p. 123). And for those countries doing the outsourcing themselves (e.g., Singapore), they need to be prepared for a loss of jobs when labor is outsourced. To prepare for those losses, Thangavelu and Chongvilaivan (2013) recommend instituting training programs to reskill people who lose jobs during outsourcings.

The Regional HRD ecosystem also involves constant learning and adaptation because it is constantly intertwined with other areas of national and regional development. Consider current efforts to promote skill development in the fishing industry given its importance to Southeast Asia. Efforts in one area are intertwined with "social dimensions of sustainability, including issues such as well-being, human rights and gender equality," which, unfortunately, "have historically been largely overlooked" (Bush et al., 2018, pp. 316–317).

HRD itself is emblematic and reflective of the process of learning and change. HRD has a role in facilitating regional talent management, especially for global organizations and multinational corporations (MNCs) in Southeast Asia. As Kim and McLean (2012) discuss, global organizations can use a mix of HRD strategies that are both centralized around the headquarters and also decentralized and autonomous within subsidiaries. Organizations can also create structured development systems aligned with strategic priorities that include cross-cultural training and strategic planning of global assignments to support leadership development in organizations (Kim & McLean, 2012).

6.4 A Case Study of the Interconnected Nature of Regional HRD

Community-based organizations (CBOs) in Myanmar (Burma) provide an illustrative case of the process of these process dimensions within the Regional HRD ecosystem. Over 214,000 CBOs designed to serve the humanitarian and educational needs of communities emerged throughout Myanmar over the last 30 years as a result of military rule and ongoing conflict among the country's ethnic groups (Steinberg, 2013; Ware, 2012). These organizations represent collective, bottom-up approaches by individuals and communities to address their needs in the face of failed social support systems, educational systems, and healthcare systems. While many bright and passionate individuals work tirelessly in their communities to bring about positive change, there is "a major human resources challenge" in the country (Crocco & Cseh, 2021, p. 437). This challenge is largely the result of poor educational systems, few opportunities for skill development, and an unstable economic environment. However, many individuals and communities have sought out ways to improve their situation by developing their knowledge and skills.

This human resource challenge is also related to Myanmar's integration into ASEAN. According to Thuzar (2013), for Myanmar to reap the benefits of the ASEAN Economic Community, it is important to "improv[e] Myanmar's human resources base to support implementation of the reforms (the country currently has a very limited talent pool of organizational, managerial and marketing skills)" (p. 208).

While living and working in Thailand, I had the opportunity to participate in one collective effort to address this challenge on the Thailand–Myanmar Border: the Project for Local Empowerment. The project was a 40 million USD project funded by the United States Agency for International Development (USAID). The project was awarded to the International Rescue Committee (IRC) in partnership with the Mae Tao Clinic in Mae Sot, the Border Consortium, and World Education (a Canadian development organization), all of which serve development needs in Myanmar and along the Thailand–Myanmar border. According to Lindgren et al. (2015), the overarching purpose of the Project for Local Empowerment, which began in 2012, was to "provide humanitarian assistance/protection services in ways that strengthen local capacities of CBOs to deliver essential services, promote collaboration and coordination across organizations, empower innate capabilities of communities, and strengthen local decision-making" (p. 14). Embedded in this initiative was a focus on HRD at the individual and organizational levels via capacity building, but it also included strengthening networks, which were shown to be a vital component of an HRD ecosystem in previous chapters.

My involvement came while I was working at Payap University. IRC sought out Payap University as a higher education partner to develop a certificate program in organizational development that would be offered to leaders and workers in CBOs along the border and in Myanmar. The certificate program as a whole was an HRD-related project and included courses such as Ethical Leadership Skills, Non-Profit Operations and Human Resource Management, and Project Management. The certificate program culminated in an applied project in organizational development, in which participants developed the content from the courses into a meaningful deliverable for their organizations. The courses in the certificate program were co-developed by Payap University faculty members and Burmese IRC development workers to ensure cultural and subject-matter relevance to the CBOs. To implement the certificate program, a Training of Trainers (ToT) program was held in which the course designers (Payap faculty members and IRC development workers) trained a set of Burmese CBO leaders to deliver the courses. Slideshows, course materials, and course sequences were provided to trainers, who then presented the courses over the weekends to participants. Participants from over 100 CBOs along the border and in several locations in Myanmar received certificates, which were especially significant given that reputable higher education credentials, like a university certificate, are difficult to attain in that context. Wherever the certificate program was offered, members from Payap and IRC conducted evaluation and quality assurance visits.

One organization that we studied (Crocco & Cseh, 2021) was itself an educational training organization that offered courses in a variety of subjects to young people in Myanmar. In this case, the leader of the organization had participated in the ToT program along the border and several of his employees had participated in the certificate program. Their participation enabled them to not only incorporate their learning into their work as a training organization, but also to offer the certificate program to other people working in CBOs in the area. Payap University continued to conduct quality assurance of the certificate's delivery at this location and deliver certificates to those who completed the required courses and application project.

This case illustrates the interconnection of the content and process dimensions of the Regional HRD ecosystem. In terms of the content dimensions, the certificate program's development and delivery was embedded within the cultural and political context of both Myanmar and Thailand. Government regulations in Myanmar influenced the delivery of the HRD effort in that they made it difficult to work directly within Myanmar. While we were able to travel there for evaluation visits, remaining connected was challenging and the policy environment was constantly changing. The political context generally in Myanmar was the reason this human resource challenge existed in the first place (e.g., poor social support and educational systems). The government regulations in Thailand also played a role, especially as they related to migration. While some look kindly on what Thailand has done along the border, more could clearly be done in terms of support for the refugees and other displaced people who live there.

Payap University as an educational institution played a key role in the design, evaluation, and conferral of the certificate. However, it worked with international partners such as IRC and its non-Southeast Asian faculty members to create the program. Faculty members at Payap

University included Thai nationals, as well as several westerners from the United States, the United Kingdom, and the Netherlands, who worked in conjunction with the Burmese workers employed by the IRC to develop the content of the courses. This process itself reflects convergence in the broader sense of a melding of the more academic conceptualizations and positionality of the Payap faculty members with the more locally derived knowledge and practice-based perspective of the development workers. Peer networks also played a role in the selection of Payap as the partner institution through social connections between the IRC development workers and Payap.

Peer networks also played a role in the selection of Payap as the partner institution through social connections between the IRC development workers and Payap. The ToT offered yet another point of divergence because the ToT workers would often deliver the course content in Burmese, which was more commonly used than English among many of the CBO workers. While the slides were in English, the trainers facilitated the class sessions in Burmese. Then, as the participants developed their own projects to apply to their organizations, they would further adapt the certificate's content to the needs of their communities and the particularities of their organizations. Peer networks were even more influential in the classes when organizational leaders were able to share with one another their various application projects, so they could continually learn from one another. As we observed in this organization, processes of social learning, i.e., learning by observing the role-modeling of others, can occur when one or more members of the organization embodies learning from the certificate program and is thus able to share that learning with other members of the organization and community. While this organization only involved two countries directly (Thailand and Myanmar), it was connected broadly to the rest of Southeast Asia via ASEAN and efforts at regional integration.

6.5 A Holistic Framework for the ASEAN Community

This chapter concludes by synthesizing the ecosystems perspective, presenting a holistic framework of Regional HRD for the ASEAN Community. This framework provides the reader with an illustration of the many components discussed in this book. It shows the macro, meso, and micro dimensions of the Regional HRD ecosystem as well as the connections with the processes of emergence, convergence and divergence, and adaptation (see Fig. 6.1). Ecosystems are a unit of both living and environmental entities. As such, they are always in a state of flux. While no two-dimensional figure can fully capture this complexity, this figure attempts to present the ecosystem as a framework to support the reader's learning and understanding. The lines around all three dimensions are permeable, a permeability meant to signify the continual shifting, melding, and overlap that occurs. The circular arrow represents the process dimensions as they move like a constant current through the content dimensions of the ecosystem.

The three circles are meant to describe the closeness to the actual activities of HRD. Individual workers, employees, and organizations are the clearest end goal of HRD. In this dimension it is HRD for "me" in the sense that HRD serves the individuals and the individual organizations and their personal and organizational goals. The meso dimension makes up components that implement HRD policy and practice but it is not at the same level of directness when compared to individual workers and organizations. For example, in this micro dimension, when an organization or local unit implements an HRD intervention of some kind, they

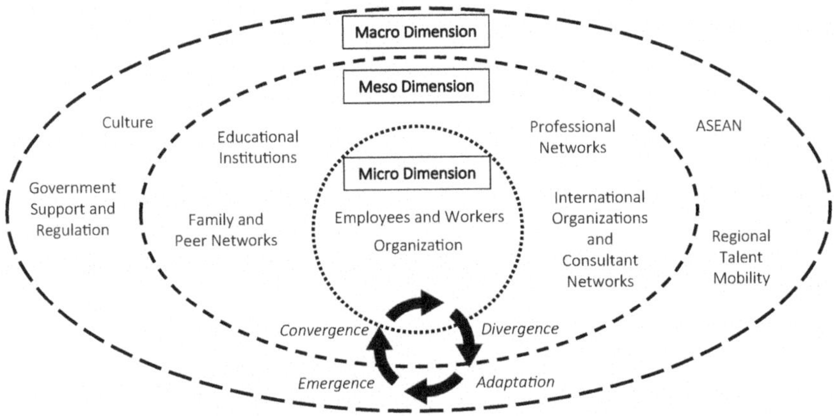

Fig. 6.1 The regional HRD ecosystem of Southeast Asia (*Note* All content and process dimensions of the Regional HRD ecosystem in Southeast Asia are constantly influenced by political, economic, social, technological, environmental, and legal forces)

are doing so in the hopes that the impact of that intervention will positively affect the organization. This is that closeness and directness that is not felt in the meso dimension. Even though universities and TVET institutions in the meso dimension are directly conducting HRD, they are not doing so to impact their own organizational outcomes but rather as an investment in larger society. That said, higher education institutions (meso dimension) or even governments for that matter (macro dimension) might conduct some kind of HRD-related professional development for their employees much like any other organization, which would resemble the micro dimension; however, in general they are operating further away from individuals in that they are having a broader and less direct impact on individuals in the ecosystem. The components of the macro dimension are even further away from the central actors of the micro dimension but still support and regulate HRD broadly.

As noted below the figure, all content and process dimensions of the Regional HRD ecosystem in Southeast Asia are constantly influenced by political, economic, social, technological, environmental, and legal forces. While these forces do not have a particular label within the figure presented here, they are inextricably tied to the evolution and processes of the Regional HRD ecosystem. The constant current of change within the Regional HRD ecosystem is propelled by a host of drivers such as strategic trust in the region, nation-state autonomy, firm autonomy, connectivity, political security, and the value of people and human rights. Mechanisms for bringing about this change include regional and subregional level policies and declarations with affiliated roadmaps and action plans, national and organizational investment in HRD, and availability of training and development opportunities for individuals. This leads to continual change in the Regional HRD ecosystem in terms of regional workforce development, labor force productivity, and overall human development and human flourishing. While not explored in depth here, each of these components is worth considering as an influence on the larger system. In this sense, developing human resources the ASEAN way is always something that will occur in a complex set of interactions and influences across these dimensions. The 11 countries and their national governments, even as 10 of them operate together within ASEAN, will continue to be important players in the regulation, funding, and supporting of HRD. ASEAN as a regional organization will continue to place a significant collaborative and facilitative role as well. But at the end of the day, HRD lives and breathes at the micro level of individual workers, employees, and organizations.

Bibliography

Acharya, A. (1998). Culture, security, multilateralism. The 'ASEAN way' and regional order. *Contemporary Security Policy, 19*(1), 55–84. https://doi.org/10.1080/13523269808404179.

Acharya, A. (2012). *The making of Southeast Asia: International relations of a region*. Cornell University Press.

Allison, L. (2015). *The EU, ASEAN and interregionalism: Regionalism support and norm diffusion between the EU and ASEAN*. Palgrave Macmillan.

Association of Southeast Asian Nations. (2018). *Handbook: ASEAN mutual recognition arrangements on tourism professionals 2018* (2nd ed.). https://asean.org/storage/2012/05/ASEAN-MRA-TP-Handbook-2nd-Edition-2018.pdf.

Association of Southeast Asian Nations. (2020a). *ASEAN declaration on human resources development for the changing world of work and its roadmap*. https://asean.org/storage/ASEAN-Declaration-on-Human-Resources-Development-for-the-Changing-World-of-Work-and-its-Roadmap_Final_19Feb2021.pdf.

Association of Southeast Asian Nations. (2020b). *ASEAN statistical yearbook 2020*. https://www.aseanstats.org/wp-content/uploads/2020/12/ASYB_2020.pdf.

Avery, G. C., & Bergsteiner, H. (Eds.). (2016). *Sufficiency thinking: Thailand's gift to an unsustainable world*. Allen & Unwin.

Bartlett, K. R., Lawler, J. J., Bae, J., Chen, S. J., & Wan, D. (2002). Differences in international human resource development among indigenous firms and multinational affiliates in East and Southeast Asia. *Human Resource Development Quarterly, 13*(4), 383–405. https://doi.org/10.1002/hrdq.1040.

Bouchon, F., & Rawat, K. (2016). Rural areas of ASEAN and tourism services, a field for innovative solutions. *Procedia—Social and Behavioral Sciences, 224*(2016), 44–51. https://doi.org/10.1016/j.sbspro.2016.05.398.

Budhwar, P., & Debrah, Y. (2009). Future research on human resource management systems in Asia. *Asia Pacific Journal of Management, 26*(2), 197–218. https://doi.org/10.1007/s10490-008-9103-6.

Bush, S. R., Marschke, M. J., & Belton, B. (2018). Labor, social sustainability and the underlying vulnerabilities of work in Southeast Asia's seafood value chains. In A. McGregor, L. Law, & F. Miller (Eds.), *Routledge handbook of Southeast Asian development* (pp. 316–329). Routledge.

Crocco, O. S., & Bunwirat, N. (2014). English in ASEAN: Key effects. *International Journal of the Computer, the Internet and Management, 22*(2), 22–27.

Crocco, O. S., & Cseh, M. (2021). Learning, development, and change in a community-based enterprise in Myanmar. *European Journal of Training and Development, 45*(4/5), 436–448.

Crocco, O. S., & Tkachenko, O. (2020). Regional human resource development: The case of Southeast Asia and ASEAN. *Human Resource Development International*. https://doi.org/10.1080/13678868.2020.1858261.

Deyo, F. C. (2006). South-East Asian industrial labour: Structural demobilisation and political transformation. In G. Rogan, K. Hewison, & R. Robison (Eds.), *The political economy of South-East Asia: Markets, power and contestation* (3rd ed., pp. 283–304). Oxford University Press.

Gam, H. T. (2021). Solutions for the human resource development cooperation for tourism in the Mekong Sub-Region. *Journal of Contemporary Issues in Business and Government, 27*(2), 4168–4173. https://doi.org/10.47750/cibg.2021.27.02.436.

Garavan, T., McCarthy, A., & Carbery, R. (2019). An ecosystems perspective on international human resource development: A meta-synthesis of the literature. *Human Resource Development Review, 18*(2), 248–288. https://doi.org/10.1177/1534484319828865.

Hou, A. Y. C., Ince, M., Tsai, S., & Chiang, C. L. (2015). Quality assurance of quality assurance agencies from an Asian perspective: Regulation, autonomy and accountability. *Asia Pacific Education Review, 16*, 95–106. https://doi.org/10.1007/s12564-015-9358-9.

Hou, A. Y. C., Hill, C., Chen, K. H., Tsai, S., & Chen, V. (2017). A comparative study of student mobility programs in SEAMEO-RIHED, UMAP, and Campus Asia: Regulation, challenges, and impacts on higher education regionalization. *Higher Education Evaluation and Development, 11*(1), 12–24. https://doi.org/10.1108/HEED-08-2017-003.

Human Resources Online. (n.d.). *Welcome to the Human Resources Online conferences homepage*. https://conferences.humanresourcesonline.net/southeast-asia/.

Jones, L., & Hameiri, S. (2020). Southeast Asian regional governance: Political economy, regulatory regionalism and ASEAN integration. In T. Carroll, S. Hameiri, & L. Jones (Eds.), *The political economy of Southeast Asia: Politics and uneven development under hyperglobalisation* (4th ed., pp. 199–224). Palgrave Macmillan.

Kenny, M., & Kinsella, M. (2015). *Policy making in adult education: A comparative approach across 21 EU regions*. http://mural.maynoothuniversity.ie/7877/1/Regional_Project_Country%20Rrofile%20Ireland_2015-10-06.pdf.

Kim, S., & McLean, G. N. (2012). Global talent management: Necessity, challenges, and the roles of HRD. *Advances in Developing Human Resources, 14*(4), 566–585. https://doi.org/10.1177/1523422312455610.

Kontogeorgopoulos, N. (2003). Towards a Southeast Asian model of resort-based 'mass ecotourism': Evidence from Phuket, Thailand and Bali, Indonesia. *ASEAN Journal on Hospitality and Tourism, 2*(1), 1–16.

Krapohl, S. (Ed.). (2017). *Regional integration in the global south*. Palgrave Macmillan.

Lindgren, D., Kitthananan, A., Khruemanee, C., Ratnawulan, D., Onsrithong, K., Panritdam, V., & Bak, M. L. (2015, January 5). *Performance evaluation of the Project for Local Empowerment (PLE) on the Thai-Burma border*. http://pdf.usaid.gov/pdf_docs/PA00KVCZ.pdf.

Mongsawad, P. (2010). The philosophy of the sufficiency economy: A contribution to the theory of development. *Asia-Pacific Development Journal, 17*(1), 123–143. https://doi.org/10.18356/02bd5fb3-en.

Novelli, M., Klatte, N., & Dolezal, C. (2017). The ASEAN community-based tourism standards: Looking beyond certification. *Tourism Planning & Development, 14*(2), 260–281. https://doi.org/10.1080/21568316.2016.1243146.

Payap University. (n.d.). *Center for social impact*. https://csi.payap.ac.th.

Pham, V. P. Q., & Thirumaran, K. (2016). Managing development of resort destinations in Southeast Asia: Emerging and peripheral Phu Quoc Island. In P. Mandal & J. Vong (Eds.), *Development of tourism and the hospitality industry in Southeast Asia* (pp. 83–95). Springer.

Rowley, C. (2017). Whither globalisation and convergence? Asian examples and future research. *Asia Pacific Business Review, 23*(1), 1–9. https://doi.org/10.1080/13602381.2016.1238602.

Rowley, C., & Benson, J. (2002). Convergence and divergence in Asian human resource management. *California Management Review, 44*(2), 90–109.

Southeast Asian Ministers of Education Organization. (n.d.-a). *History*. https://www.seameo.org/Main_about/89.

Southeast Asian Ministers of Education Organization. (n.d.-b). *7 priority areas*. https://www.seameo.org/Main_programme/189.

Srisaeng, P., & Upvall, M. J. (2020). Looking toward 2030: Strengthening midwifery education through regional partnerships. *Journal of Advanced Nursing, 76*(2), 715–724. https://doi.org/10.1111/jan.14015.

Steinberg, D. I. (2013). *Burma/Myanmar: What everyone needs to* know (2nd ed.). Oxford University Press.

Te, V., Griffiths, R., Law, K., Hill, P. S., & Annear, P. L. (2018). The impact of ASEAN economic integration on health worker mobility: A scoping review of the literature. *Health Policy and Planning, 33*(8), 957–965. https://doi.org/10.1093/heapol/czy071.

Thangavelu, S., & Chongvilaivan, A. (2013). *Globalization, outsourcing, and labor development in ASEAN*. Routledge.

Thuzar, M. (2013). Myanmar in the ASEAN economic community: Preparing for the future. In S. Basu Das (Ed.), *ASEAN economic community scorecard*. ISEAS—Yusof Ishak Institute.

Umemiya, N. (2008). Regional quality assurance activity in higher education in Southeast Asia: Its characteristics and driving forces. *Quality in Higher Education, 14*(3), 277–290. https://doi.org/10.1080/13538320802507679.

Ware, A. (2012). *Context-sensitive development: How international NGOs operate in Myanmar.* Kumarian Press.

Warner, M., & Rowley, C. (2007). Conclusion: Whither business and management in South East Asia? In C. Rowley & M. Warner (Eds.), *Management in South-East Asia* (pp. 175–181). Routledge.

Wong, E. P. Y., Mistilis, N., & Dywer, L. (2011). A framework for analyzing intergovernmental collaboration: The case of ASEAN tourism. *Tourism Management, 32*(2), 367–376. https://doi.org/10.1016/j.tourman.2010.03.006.

Yeates, N. (2019). World regional social governance, policy and development. In J. Midgley, R. Surender, & L. Alfers (Eds.), *Handbook of Social Policy and Development* (pp. 224–245). Edward Elgar Publishing Ltd.

CHAPTER 7

The Future of HRD in Southeast Asia

This chapter returns to Natalegawa's (2018) question posed at the beginning of this book: "How can ASEAN become more relevant to the peoples of ASEAN, such that its contributions can be genuinely felt in making better the lives of its citizens?" (p. 1). HRD at the individual, organizational, national, and regional levels has the opportunity to improve the lives of Southeast Asian citizens, but many questions remain. This chapter takes into consideration several of the key criticisms and concerns regarding Regional HRD. It then offers a set of implications for future research, policy, and practice to deepen and expand understanding about this Regional HRD ecosystem.

7.1 Critiques and Questions

7.1.1 *Challenges of ASEAN and the ASEAN Way*

First, it is important to examine the role of ASEAN in HRD. While ASEAN has made great strides in supporting regional interactions and engaging collectively with partners outside of the region (Natalegawa, 2018), perhaps its biggest contribution has been its focus on the people of Southeast Asia. This people-centric view has intensified in ASEAN as many of the immediate political and security challenges facing Southeast Asian countries at its inception began to abate or at least shift. The

O. S. Crocco, *Developing Human Resources in Southeast Asia*, Palgrave Macmillan Asian Business Series,
https://doi.org/10.1007/978-3-030-79697-6_7

people-centric view is also the result of ASEAN's increasing influence in the region through its 2008 ASEAN Charter and the ASEAN Community Blueprint of its tripartite communities (socio-cultural, political, and economic). While clear efforts have been made to strengthen the region by developing its people, many questions remain.

One of these questions concerns the organization's ability to embrace other stakeholders within the region as true partners. For example, in its attempt to be "people-oriented," ASEAN has only recently begun to engage civil society organizations (CSOs) in Southeast Asia as meaningful stakeholders (Gerard, 2014). CSOs play an important role in Regional HRD as actors outside of the state who contribute to dialogue about human rights, political engagement, and labor relations. But has ASEAN's engagement with CSOs been authentic? Gerard (2014) argues that "ASEAN's attempts to include CSOs in policymaking have not been a neutral, [or] benign, reform" (p. 155). She goes on to say that "ASEAN's attempt to pluralize policymaking through the inclusion of CSOs is directed toward re-legitimating ASEAN's political project, rather than establishing channels for CSOs to deliberate policy" (p. 156). In this sense, the engagement could be perceived as only quasi-inclusive given the "alliances between domestic cartels and political elites that have developed over the course of the region's rapid industrialization," which have inhibited CSOs' abilities to influence policy and practice (Gerard, 2014, p. 160). While the work of CSOs is not always directly related to HRD, the example of HRD provides insight into how challenging it would be for various actors to influence policymaking regionally. This example also begs the question of whether ASEAN's attempts to include an array of stakeholders in policymaking, especially as the latter relates to HRD, are genuine and/or if other actors have too much influence to make it a reality. As one longtime Southeast Asian scholar notes, until now, ASEAN has not exactly been used as a vehicle for democratization (Emmerson, 2007).

Some authors wonder if placing ASEAN on such a pedestal represents nothing more than "ideological faith" at best and damaging "delusion" at worst (Jones & Smith, 2006, p. 2). The delusion even extends to the idea of shared values in ASEAN as it relates to the ASEAN Way (Jones & Smith, 2006). The most glaring critique of ASEAN made in various contexts and at different times concerns human rights violations and autocratic regimes in the region (Weatherbee, 2019). Many of these criticisms are worthy of attention, especially given ASEAN's weak response to recent events such as the Rohingya crisis and the 2021 military coup in Myanmar. At the heart of this criticism lies the efficacy of the ASEAN Way, which espouses non-interference and consensual decision-making. Jones (2012) has critiqued the constructivist view that ASEAN operates under a principle of non-interference based on the fact that it "operates selectively" (p. 8), as shown by the counterexamples of Indonesia's annexation of Timor-Leste in 1975 and Vietnam's invasion of Cambodia in 1978. Invoking the phrase used by Krasner (1999), Jones labels the principle of non-interference "organized hypocrisy" (p. 211). Even at ASEAN's most recent summit in April 2021, concerning Myanmar after the military coup, the five points of consensus failed to stipulate the release of political prisoners or establish follow-up meetings or measures to ensure the fulfillment of the items agreed upon (ASEAN, 2021).

ASEAN clearly is an important actor in the Regional HRD ecosystem and these criticisms of the organization and the ASEAN Way have implications for establishing better channels for Regional HRD to thrive. In the face of continual political and technological changes, Tan Sri Datuk Dr. Rebecca Fatima Sta. Maria (2018) of the Economic Research Institute for ASEAN and East Asia (ERIA) has said, "ASEAN must be bold and dynamic… less sanguine." It may even need to renegotiate how it utilizes its cherished ASEAN Way.

7.1.2 *Challenges to Regionalism*

No ecosystem exists in complete isolation from external forces. Even the extent to which an ecosystem is enclosed is in itself an influence on the boundaries of that ecosystem. For example, Crocco and Tkachenko (2020) have expounded elsewhere on the influence of extra-regional partners on Regional HRD, not as direct components of the Regional HRD ecosystem per se, but through funding HRD projects, hosting training, and influencing policy. There are many other challenges to regionalism generally in Southeast Asia that threaten the stability of the region and its ability to collaborate economically, politically, and culturally. These include, but are certainly not limited to, the aforementioned Rohingya crisis in Myanmar, which posed a significant policy challenge for ASEAN and regional integration even before the coup (Roberts, 2010; Than, 2005); the South China Sea; trade regimes that privilege some Southeast Asian countries over others, such as the Comprehensive and Progressive

Agreement for the Trans-Pacific Partnerships; and the U.S.-China trade war (Buszynski, 2019).

Of particular note is the rising influence of China in the region, which has the potential to challenge regional stability. A divide is emerging between Southeast Asian countries that align themselves with China and those more skeptical of Chinese influence (M. Cook, 2018). The closeness of Cambodia and Lao PDR with China has caused some people, such as Singaporean diplomat Bilahari Kausikan (2020), to even question whether those countries can be meaningful members of ASEAN. Given that all decisions in ASEAN are made by consensus, by influencing the positions of Cambodia and Lao PDR, China could effectively veto any decision that would otherwise solidify the region against it. The divide in loyalty to China has potential implications for HRD in terms of qualification frameworks and the cultural ideology surrounding HRD policy and practice. On the other end of the spectrum, this divide could lead to major strains within ASEAN and potentially become a threat to regional security.

Another notable concern related to the Regional HRD ecosystem is the impact of Timor-Leste's exclusion from full membership in ASEAN. As a member of the region as a whole, Timor-Leste's lack of influence in ASEAN continues to damage the country's overall progress (Hägerdal & Berlie, 2018) as well as its ability to integrate into the regional economy. In the short term, the economic ramifications of its exclusion were primarily contained within its borders. In the long term, however, its status as an outcast may also negatively affect Regional HRD, particularly in countries geographically close to Timor-Leste.

Refugees and human trafficking also threaten regionalism. While ASEAN has attempted to support refugees, only Cambodia and the Philippines are signatories on the UN Refugee Convention. Several other countries in Southeast Asia view refugees more as undocumented labor or as the result of human trafficking and have neglected to implement the needed support structures (Tubakovic, 2019). ASEAN regional mechanisms, such as the ASEAN Intergovernmental Commission on Human Rights and the ASEAN Human Rights Declaration, are important steps in the right direction; however, they still lack the enforcement needed to expedite support. This issue has a direct influence on Regional HRD, as employment and workplace safety are essential components of supporting people in those vulnerable groups.

7.1.3 *A Region of Diversity*

At face value, it would appear that at least the ideals of collective benefit and humanism are in effect in the Southeast Asian context, especially because a more developed workforce is linked to working conditions and human rights. The ASEAN (2001) publication "Preparing workers for changes in the labour market" entails that "investments in appropriate training to increase employability be accompanied by measures to ensure that decent working conditions are brought about, since productivity, creativity, as well as innovation – requires a sense of freedom, dignity, and equality at the workplace" (p. 37). This statement raises a host of questions within the unique political, economic, and cultural framework of Southeast Asia concerning how individual organizations and governments are aiding or suppressing this progress.

As discussed in previous chapters, cultural and political diversity shape the Regional HRD ecosystem. While often an asset, this diversity can also become a challenge for ASEAN. Deep-seated nationalism, the lack of an enforcement mechanism, and the expansion of large, state-based corporations are all challenges that face ASEAN in general (Balakrishnan, 2017), but also influence Regional HRD. For example, nationalism could affect the attainment of effective talent mobility in a variety of ways. A strong national identity, like that found in Thailand, could make it difficult for Thai workers to smoothly integrate into another country's workforce, as was found by Pruetipibultham (2019). Strong nationalism could also influence the receiving country's willingness to adopt policies that invest in those workers.

There is the possibility, however, that attempts to educate and standardize HRD policies and practices regionally restrict and ignore ethnic diversity. As mentioned in Chapter 3, Southeast Asia is incredibly diverse with hundreds of ethnic minority groups and indigenous communities throughout the region (Turner, 2018). The focus on regional identity building, largely as a reaction against the legacy of colonialism in the region, has meant that nationalism (and subsequently a regionalism built on countries), has dominated the conversation. ASEAN and other regional leaders seem to be satisfied with framing diversity as it pertains to multiple national cultures but not as it pertains to the hundreds of ethnic minority and indigenous populations. If this trend continues, efforts at developing the region's workforce have the potential to stamp out important cultural differences and local wisdom in the name of standardization.

7.1.4 A Region of Disparities

To some, a book about Regional HRD would appear to be an addition to the body of literature that generally does not investigate the role of the authoritarian regimes of the region in the historic atrocities that have occurred. While I have sought to educate myself through relationships and readings, this book does at times read as an appreciative inquiry of the very positive aspects of HRD as opposed to its shortcomings (Coghlan et al., 2003). That said, it would not be a complete analysis if it did not include a discussion about real criticisms concerning disparities in the region.

There are a host of regional disparities at the national, organizational, and individual levels related to and affecting Regional HRD. For example, there are incredible gender disparities that favor males over females in areas such as adult literacy rates and unemployment rates (ASEAN, 2020a). Southeast Asian governments offer a variety of systems to develop women as leaders. However, according to an analysis of the number of women in national-level legislatures, the country with the highest proportion of women is the Philippines at 29.5%, while the lowest is Brunei at just 9.1% (ASEAN, 2020a). This disparity matters for Regional HRD because the more women have an equitable seat when writing national legislation, the more their interests can be balanced with men's. This disparity also matters in terms of reaching the United Nations Sustainable Development Goals. The Southeast Asian countries with the highest proportions of women in managerial roles are the Philippines (52.7%), Brunei (41.1%), and Singapore (37.9%), while Cambodia and Myanmar report the lowest proportions, at less than 1% (ASEAN, 2020b).

At the national level, economic disparities remain within many, if not all, of the Southeast Asian countries. These inequities are documented in countries such as the Philippines (Andriesse, 2017), where "poor households cannot afford to pay for skills training" (p. 100). In the case of the Philippines, the disparity in education and skills training is largely due to "local political dynasties" that monopolize funding and do not prioritize HRD (Andriesse, 2017, p. 106). This absence of HRD can be seen in disparities between Southeast Asia's high-income and low to middle-income countries. Whereas every Singaporean citizen has access to training and development opportunities through the online skill development website mentioned previously, many citizens in Myanmar, Lao PDR, Cambodia, and Timor-Leste do not even have access to the Internet much less higher education. According to Freedom House (n.d.), Vietnam, Myanmar, and Thailand all score "Not Free" in terms of Internet freedom, which considers access, limits on content, and violations of users' rights. While Internet access might seem only tangentially related to HRD, it is, in fact, integral, given that massive open online courses (MOOCs) and other online learning opportunities are crucial to the HRD of individuals.

At the individual level, migrant workers are marginalized and taken advantage of and/or discriminated against based on gender, age, and appearance (Kathiravelu & Wong, 2019). Similarly, people who have been trafficked within the region or who have such little access to resources that they cannot even consider building on their skills are also discriminated against.

These disparities will be exacerbated by the changing nature of work. The fourth industrial revolution and the associated technological advancements will massively disrupt HRD and skill development more broadly (Ra et al., 2019). For example, in countries such as Indonesia, Thailand, and Vietnam, the demand for jobs requiring manual labor has decreased, while the demand for jobs that involve "nonroutine and cognitive tasks" has increased (Ra et al., 2019, p. 28). Technological advancements will also ease outsourcing and increase competition for labor both in regional markets and beyond, as the workforce is now globally competitive. Production services have also become streamlined and/or automated, widening the digital divide between those with access to technology and those without. While small- and medium-sized enterprises (SMEs) are a vital part of job creation and economic development, SMEs rarely have resources to devote toward training (Short & Gray, 2018). However, most learning and training occurs on the job. With respect to this latter issue, ASEAN and the Southeast Asian governments can step in and support SMEs via training programs. ASEAN (2015) outlines some strategies in this regard, which is certainly a major area of growth for the region.

HRD has been one of the key policy recommendations for closing the development gap between ASEAN's high/upper-middle-income countries and its low-income ones precisely because it is interconnected to so many aspects of society and well-being. Carpenter and McGillivray (2013) write, "ASEAN supports achievements in human capital in a number of ways, through human resource development of government officials working in health and education, the training of higher education officials, student exchanges through the ASEAN University Network (AUN), and various health sector initiatives that focus on communicable diseases and physical activity" (p. 185). They go on to advocate that the region should not only prioritize HRD but also commit to HRD actions that will bring about the desired goals, in particular as they relate to the ASEAN Socio-Cultural Community (Carpenter & McGillivray, 2013). As the world continues to change due to globalization, technological advancements, and political disruption, HRD has the potential to either exacerbate or ameliorate existing disparities.

7.1.5 *National and Regional HRD: Do They Exist?*

A final major critique worth discussing is the notion that the concept of National HRD (NHRD)—and by extension Regional HRD, although not mentioned explicitly—is conceptually unclear and/or redundant in academic scholarship (e.g., Wang, 2008; Wang & Swanson, 2008). Is Regional HRD a verifiable concept or is it merely a repackaging of HRD for a regional context? McLean et al. (2008) have responded directly to this question as it relates to NHRD, as McLean, a major proponent of the usefulness of the concept of NHRD, has conducted many studies and projects related to HRD in Southeast Asia (e.g., Tran et al., 2021). Wang et al. (2017) have put forth a compelling definition of HRD, which, interestingly, has not found its way into an HRD journal, as "a mechanism in shaping individual and group values and beliefs and skilling through learning-related activities to support the desired performance of the host system" (p. 1175). This definition highlights the four components of HRD as a *mechanism* involving the acts of *shaping* and *skilling* at the direction of a *host system*. In this sense, it is possible to look at a region like Southeast Asia or, even more easily, at a regional organization like ASEAN as a host system.

The idea of the host system is the "defining attribute" of HRD according to Wang et al. (2017, p. 1172); however, it is precisely this component that an ecosystems perspective might be seen as rejecting. While Wang et al. (2017) employ a systems thinking approach, they always return to the host system as the autonomous agent that guides or at least influences HRD processes. However, in the case of a Regional HRD ecosystem, there is no autonomous agent that serves as the host system. In the case of Southeast Asia, ASEAN definitely has a powerful role in the regional coordination of HRD activities and certainly has played a role in the emergence of the ecosystem as discussed above; however, if Timor-Leste is also to be included in the region, then the regional ecosystem supersedes ASEAN. In this sense, there is no governing body or institution that sets the complete agenda for Regional HRD or has full power over the ecosystem. It is a collage of actors and forces. The risk, of course, is that those with more power use their influence to bend HRD to their purposes, which may or may not have the best interests of all the region's citizens in mind. In this sense, the host system is more a feature of a Regional HRD ecosystem rather than a counterexample.

7.2 Implications for HRD Research

A driving impetus for this book was the desire to provide scholars, practitioners, policymakers, and students with a starting point that fuels a robust research agenda and sets best practices for studying ASEAN and developing human resources in Southeast Asia. As a result, this section discusses applications of this analysis to future HRD research. The implications for future research are centered around further exploration of the individual components and relationships within the Regional HRD ecosystem, further contextualization of the study of HRD within Southeast Asian, and further research on Regional HRD using alternate viewpoints and methodologies.

7.2.1 Diving Deeper into the Regional HRD Ecosystem

While this book has provided an overview of the Regional HRD ecosystem in Southeast Asia, in some ways it has raised more questions than it has answered. Consider the following selection of questions related to each dimension.

The macro dimension:

- Do cultural value dimensions, either from the GLOBE studies or from Hofstede, do a disservice to the study of the Regional HRD ecosystem by overemphasizing national-level differences?
- What are the relationships between national, ethnic, and organizational cultures in Southeast Asia?

- While we have some insight into countries like Vietnam and Singapore, how are government policies influencing HRD in the meso and micro dimensions of the ecosystem, and vice versa?
- While we know about ASEAN-level policies, declarations, and programs related to HRD, what has been the impact of these on HRD policy and practice at the individual, organizational, and national levels? What evaluation studies have been conducted in this area?
- How could the region use HRD to further support regional talent mobility, especially in the cases of migrant workers, refugees, and other vulnerable populations? What are the best practices in this area? How can the region learn from other countries/regions that have navigated this territory more effectively?
- How has ASEAN affected the boundaries of the ecosystem? What has been the impact on Regional HRD of excluding Timor-Leste from full ASEAN membership?

The meso dimension:

- What is the process of HRD knowledge transfer between international organizations or consultant networks with local Southeast Asian organizations and individuals?
- How have international development organizations influenced HRD policy and practice? To what extent is this influence permanent?
- What is the interaction between professional networks in the region and peer organizations in extra-regional countries like China, Japan, South Korea, the United States, and the United Kingdom?
- To what extent do higher education institutions influence the Regional HRD ecosystem and vice versa? How could universities better collaborate with organizations of all kinds to support Regional HRD?

The micro dimension:

- How are the gig economy and the rise of contract work influencing the attitudes, motivations, and methods of workers with respect to HRD?
- How is online learning and training being utilized and valued? What are its effects on workplace outcomes?

- What, if any, novel HRD practices exist and/or are emerging within the Southeast Asian context?

  Several other macroeconomic and extra-regional forces are worth exploring, as they influence the Regional HRD ecosystem. A couple of examples are given below:
- How will the newly signed Regional Comprehensive Economic Partnership influence subsequent HRD initiatives?
- Given that the European Union is ASEAN's biggest investor, how does this relationship influence HRD? What type of priorities related to HRD do investors seek out?

7.2.2 *The Need for Contextualization*

This initial set of questions must be contextualized in HRD research on Southeast Asia. Contextualization recognizes that social phenomena are embedded within a set of circumstances (Hantrais, 1999). Contextualization is needed because the way in which HRD occurs at the individual, organizational, national, and regional levels in Southeast Asia is a result of the unique cultural, political, and economic environment. In an analysis of strategic human resource management in Singapore, Stanton and Nankervis (2011) identify variables unique to the Singaporean context that are worth exploring, such as government imperatives or management approaches that may influence policy and practice. Consider Thailand, unique in that it is one of the only countries in the world never officially colonized. How, if at all, might this absence of colonization influence HRD policy and practice? It is also worth considering how phenomena related to HRD, such as workplace learning or career development, might express themselves differently in Southeast Asian contexts. For example, we know from research on China that cultural values such as harmony, authority, and reciprocity provide important contextualization for workplace practices (Zhu & Warner, 2019).

The most reliable source of contextualized HRD research is that which is conducted and published by Southeast Asian scholars. The representation of Southeast Asian scholars conducting original empirical research in Southeast Asian organizations is growing; however, many of these studies import research paradigms, theories, and frameworks from other contexts. Many of the scales and instruments in quantitative studies of Southeast Asian populations, even if employed by Southeast Asian scholars, were developed in largely western contexts (i.e., the United States, the

United Kingdom, and the Netherlands) (Cseh & Crocco, 2020). Take, for example, an important study by Dung and Hai (2020) on the effect of transformational leadership on the job satisfaction and commitment to organizational change of Vietnamese employees across a variety of industries. I have little doubt about the existence of universal management practices that apply across cultures as elucidated by Hamlin (2004) and subsequent studies in a variety of national contexts such as France (Hamlin & Patel, 2017), Korea (Chai et al., 2016), Mexico (Ruiz et al., 2014), and Canada (Hamlin & Whitford, 2020). However, Dung and Hai's (2020) use of the Multifactor Leadership Questionnaire (MLQ) developed by the U.S. scholars Avolio and Bass (2004) raises the question of whether the items are truly transferrable to a Southeast Asian context. At least, this question needs to be explored further before translating and applying scales developed elsewhere.

Consider the MLQ item "others have complete faith in me," which is used to describe the factor of idealized influence. Even employing sophisticated processes of translation and back-translation, having "faith" in someone in an organization could have a variety of meanings in the Southeast Asian context (which is not in itself a monolith), many of which would be difficult to tease out in such a simple sentence. In a high-power distance culture, such as those of many Southeast Asian countries, having faith in your supervisor may be a matter of obedience, which would be praised and valued. However, when compared to the espoused values of creativity needed to spur innovation as a means of competitive advantage (Ismail & Alam, 2019; Somkram, 2017), blindly following your leader would likely be counterproductive. Even within a culture such as Thailand's, the word faith is not easily translated given that the concept is largely the result of protestant Christianity and not relevant in the Thai context generally. One of the common translations of faith has to do with belief, which is generally perceived as negative given its relation to gullibility.

7.2.3 A Time for Scholarly Wandering

As scholars seek to conduct research on HRD in Southeast Asia that accounts for the unique context of the region, future research should not be constrained by conventional HRD and HRD-related research. As McLean (2010) argues, the field needs to remain open to new methodologies, theories, and strategies and push the boundaries of the field both broader and deeper in terms of the social, cultural, and even political and economic phenomena related to HRD. Thus, as researchers seek to make meaningful contributions to HRD research in the Southeast Asian context, it is important not to limit them to existing theories, frameworks, or data collection and analysis methods. In fact, as Crocco and Grenier (2021) argue, the COVID-19 global pandemic has marked a time during which HRD researchers should engage in a type of scholarly "wandering": "Wandering *away from* existing paradigms, explanations, and wandering *into* the breadth and depth of voices, perspectives, and experiences" (p. 62).

One way to facilitate this paradigmatic wandering as Crocco and Grenier (2021) recommend is through the use of autoethnography (Anderson, 2006; Ellis & Bochner, 2000), which is a methodology that involves the researcher adopting the dual role of researcher and participant. Autoethnography is a critically reflexive practice of analyzing one's experiences as data to understand a component of culture which, in the case of HRD, typically relates to culture as it emerges in organizations. There is even an organizational autoethnography (Doloriert & Sambrook, 2012) methodology, in which individuals study their experiences within organizational contexts and "explore the mundane, ignored and distorted in current academic life, past and other work experiences" (p. 90). While autoethnography itself was developed in the West, it purports to capture emic perspectives by a researcher who has, literally, first-hand knowledge of the participant. While autoethnography as it is practiced in other contexts might not apply in Southeast Asia, methodologies such as autoethnography and grounded theory that seek to explore emic phenomena from the bottom up will aid Southeast Asian scholars in conducting contextualized research.

Furthermore, as Emmerson (2020) quips, sometimes a bird's eye view on a topic requires multiple birds. Considering this, my first recommendation in this area, and perhaps the most important in this chapter, is to expand this initial seed of an idea into a project that brings together emic perspectives from all 11 Southeast Asian countries. An edited volume exploring the way in which NHRD in each of the Southeast Asian countries influences and is influenced by the Regional HRD ecosystem would provide needed insight into the interrelationships between national and regional actors. My colleagues and I attempted to begin this line of research in our chapter on Vietnam and the relationship between NHRD in Vietnam and ASEAN (Crocco et al., 2021), but more in-depth analyses of the other countries in Southeast Asia are needed. Similar to the volume edited by Engel and Mattheis (2020) on the impact of finances (e.g., budgeting, resourcing) on region-building across many regional organizations such as ASEAN, the Union of South American Nations (UNASUR), and the Caribbean Community, future research could also explore Regional HRD and its influence on region-building.

While this study was based on an ecosystems perspective of International HRD (Garavan et al., 2019), which extends beyond a systems thinking approach, other approaches could provide additional insight into this phenomenon. For example, the additional human ecology approach (Steiner, 2016) from sociology would extend the analysis to include the relationship of the HRD ecosystem with the physical world. Considering the fact that HRD is such an interdisciplinary, and even transdisciplinary, field, there are many other ways to incorporate important disciplinary insights from a wide range of scientific tools.

7.3 Implications for HRD Policy and Practice

In addition to implications for research, this study has an array of implications for HRD policy and practice across various levels of analysis. These include a focus on unity and diversity in Regional HRD, regional networking of HRD practitioners, Regional HRD to close development gaps, digital infrastructure and Regional HRD, and the ability of HRD to support a regional response to disasters.

7.3.1 The Coordination of Diversity

No one actor controls an ecosystem, which means that no single entity, even ASEAN, can orchestrate HRD in the region in its entirety. That said, there are many things ASEAN has done and can do in the future to promote a vibrant and healthy Regional HRD ecosystem. As part of the ASEAN Leaders' Statement on Human Resources and Skills Development for Economic Recovery and Sustainable Growth (ASEAN, 2012), a stated goal was to "promote sharing of experiences, best practices and knowledge in human resource development through seminars, workshops and training sessions, including the regular convening of the ASEAN Human Resource Conference" (p. 22). Building on these efforts and similar ones outlined in the ASEAN (2020c) declaration on HRD for the changing nature of work, ASEAN plays an important role in coordinating and facilitating Regional HRD efforts. While ASEAN has done a good job at creating policies and rhetoric around HRD, little information is available as to the evaluation and impact of those HRD and HRD-related initiatives.

To better coordinate HRD activities regionally, ASEAN should welcome Timor-Leste as a full member, so that any work ASEAN undertakes concerning HRD is inclusive of the entire region. According to Severino (2015), "ASEAN has no choice but to integrate the Southeast Asian economy, not only for investment and other economic reasons, but also for geo-strategic ones" (p. 21). The inclusion of Timor-Leste in this integration, as well as the actions of HRD in making the region economically vibrant, will be vital. With automation on the rise and massive job displacement looming, HRD is an increasingly pressing policy issue. To what extent should governments get involved? Should incentives be offered to companies? As Dr. Mari Pangestu in her lecture at Lee Kuan Yew School of Public Policy points out, governments are responsible for managing transitions brought about by economic disruption (Pangestu, 2019).

There are certain advantages in establishing a centralized body like a Center for Human Resource Development within ASEAN that would serve as a coordinating mechanism for all HRD-related initiatives across its three communities (Socio-Cultural, Political, and Economic). A centralized body would help disrupt the siloed nature of these three communities within ASEAN. A Center for HRD could eliminate redundancies in HRD-related efforts, identify funding for HRD projects, and ascertain HRD needs at various levels across the region. From an HRD practice standpoint, it could also coordinate between organizations, governments, and a host of other actors to identify best practices in various contexts throughout the region. Additionally, member countries could share their best practices and policies with one another, providing technical assistance and cooperation when possible. This coordination is one way in which the region could "measure and monitor gaps in education and develop strategic interventions for the sharing of best practices across ASEAN countries using triangular cooperation modalities" (Carpenter & McGillivray, 2013, p. 189), which would support the cohesion and vibrance of the Regional HRD ecosystem.

In addition, consider how a Center for HRD could influence regional talent mobility, as well as help facilitate further standardization in terms of pre-departure, post-arrival, and re-integration of cross-boundary employees. Workers who moved to a new country within the region for work would be aided by an understanding of local laws related to immigration and employment, cultural practices, and appropriate behaviors at work (ASEAN, 2001). Carpenter and McGillivray (2013) recommend that ASEAN expand labor mobility to include more than just skilled labor, thus boosting the social protection of migrant labor, ensuring that they have access to the training and skill development necessary for improving skills. A Center for HRD such as the one described here could be a place where training and development programs across a variety of industries and professions could be housed. For example, consider migrant safety, an area in which stakeholders have urged ASEAN to "consider holding a regional training course on migrants' education and safe migration campaigns" (ASEAN, 2017, p. 165). If ASEAN were to create such a training program, it could be offered online with manuals that non-ASEAN members could also use. In general, ASEAN could further aid in understanding and supporting migrant labor within the region to bring national-level practices in line with the espoused values of ASEAN.

For Southeast Asian countries to become "creative economies," they will need continued investment in areas that promote innovation such as HRD, higher education, and entrepreneurial skill development (Puutio, 2016, p. 238).The countries and ASEAN as a whole need to support lifelong learning, while recognizing it is a privilege for the wealthy. Therefore, they should provide incentives that empower individuals and SMEs to promote the learning and development of people. ASEAN has a role, especially in "improving the education and training outcomes for adults and improving regional education cooperation, particularly in technical and scientific education" (Carpenter & McGillivray, 2013, p. 188). Given the difficulties that the ASEAN member countries have had in harmonizing their labor laws (Sale, 2020), it is unlikely that harmonization of HRD would or could occur. However, ASEAN needs to lead in this regard, potentially synthesizing the countries' efforts to communicate more clearly about regional expectations, priorities, and strategies.

HRD in general, and skill development in particular, would benefit from a capacious regional conceptualization that includes not only technical skills but also cognitive and soft skills, coordinated through knowledge management systems and a regional regulatory framework (Parry & Hayden, 2015). A key component of this system would be that it be responsive to workforce needs and employer changes in desired skills and competencies, especially as technology continues to play an influential role in changing workforce competencies. Given the cultural richness of the region, HRD can play a role in "developing global competencies" for workers in global and/or cross-cultural organizations (Kim & McLean, 2012, p. 575). These competencies may include "cultural self-awareness, global perspectives, language, tolerance for ambiguity and differences, cultural flexibility, and strong communication skills" (Kim & McLean, 2012, p. 576; Marquart et al., 2004). This conceptualization would be another way in which ASEAN could lead in terms of promoting unity amid its remarkable diversity.

7.3.2 *Regional Networking of HRD Practitioners*

Considering the prominent role of professional networks, consultant networks, and peer/family networks in the Regional HRD ecosystem, one future area of development is the cultivation and exploration of these networks and their functions. Given how important professional networks are for "legitimizing HRD practices" (Garavan et al., 2019, p. 256), fostering networks of professionals within the region as a whole would help with knowledge and practice dissemination. One area ripe for major development is technical and vocational education and training (TVET). Carpenter and McGillivray (2013) write,

> ASEAN should establish a network of technical and vocational colleges and other adult education institutions to facilitate the development of common quality assurance mechanisms, standardized accreditation, student exchanges and governance strengthening initiatives. These should be linked to labour mobility initiatives and the ongoing training of skilled workers. (p. 189)

Recently, ASEAN has made great strides in TVET; however, additional networking between TVET institutions and industries is possible, as shown in Chapter 4. Similarly, networks of higher education institutions in which even departments can share information and resources as well as collaborate more closely within the region are possible. Further cultivation of networks surrounding entrepreneurs, SMEs, non-governmental organizations, and community-based organizations could provide additional platforms for knowledge sharing about HRD.

7.3.3 *Regional HRD to Close Development Gaps*

As the region seeks to close the development gap between its high-income, upper-middle-income, and lower-middle-income countries, it should do so not only in the most expedient way possible but also in the most inclusive way as possible. This sentiment was captured by Lum (2013) regarding the creation of common surgical guidelines in the region. His main contention was that a "public health approach" should be taken when establishing regional standards, taking into consideration rural and low-income areas in the region that lack a large healthcare infrastructure. What does this consideration mean for HRD? It means that as Southeast Asian countries consider common standards for surgeons, they "should target their training programmes… biased towards generality rather than sub-speciality and towards functionality rather than pre-occupation with expensive high technology techniques with marginal benefit in improving outcomes" (Lum, 2013, p. 120). This approach will allow those areas most in need to have access to capable surgeons with qualifications in line with regional standards who are also trained for general circumstances.

HRD cannot be something that is only regionally coordinated, which potentially excludes populations and sub-national focal points. Poor job quality, especially in the informal economy, means that many people lack the skills to make a living. This type of "vulnerable employment" accounts for a large percentage of low-income areas in individual Southeast Asian countries and must be addressed, especially as many of these jobs are disappearing due to economic disruption (Sakamoto, 2019, p. 71). More targeted efforts at skill development, beyond simply TVET, that reach the organizations and communities in these areas are needed to bridge this "equity divide" (Sakamoto, 2019, p. 70).

7.3.4 *Digital Infrastructure and Regional HRD*

Considering the increasing role of online training and development in the region, and the world as a whole, facilitating Regional HRD will rely on a robust Internet infrastructure. Over the last decade, Southeast Asian countries have made enormous strides in this regard. Countries such as Myanmar and Cambodia increased the percentage of their citizens who had access to the Internet from around 1% in 2010 to over a third in 2019 (ASEAN, 2020). As a whole, ASEAN member countries averaged only 18.7 Internet users for every 100 people in 2010, an average that rose to 57 in 2019 (ASEAN, 2020a). Access to the digital economy is also a matter of gender equality. As Marsan and Sey (2021) argue, there is a "digital gender divide" as well, in which women, especially those in rural areas, do not have access to basic digital technology. This divide limits access to STEM programs, which, in turn, disenfranchises women from access to high-tech skill development, higher-paying jobs, and leadership roles (Marsan & Sey, 2021). A comprehensive digital infrastructure will be a vital component of the Regional HRD ecosystem moving forward. Once a wealth of resources devoted to HRD are online, it will also be important that workers and employees have "learnability skills." In other words, being motivated and able to develop one's workplace knowledge and skills by accessing available resources will be of the utmost importance moving forward (Ra et al., 2019, p. 33).

7.3.5 Regional HRD for Disaster Relief

HRD has been shown to be a mechanism for responding to humanitarian crises and providing disaster relief in the region (A. D. B. Cook, 2018), especially given its history of natural disasters. Training has always been an important component of the region's efforts in this area (Lai et al., 2009). Even before the COVID-19 pandemic, preparing to defend against contagions "is both infrastructure and human resource intensive," and developing human resources "may be justifiably identified as an essential capacity and the one that needs the greatest attention and resource mobilization moving forward" (Davies, 2019, p. 40). While the region has made efforts to organize HRD-related initiatives in response to the pandemic, "building human resource capacity" has historically lagged behind the region's "rhetorical commitments" in this regard (p. 364).

7.4 Concluding Remarks

The boundaries of HRD as a field of academic study and professional practice are expanding. In the face of global challenges, HRD scholars and practitioners are compelled to engage with new complex socio-cultural, political, and economic realities. National HRD has been an important contribution to the HRD literature and has represented a key expansion of the field. This study adds to that literature and shows that Regional HRD can be analyzed from an ecosystems perspective and that this approach offers insight into the actors, forces, and networks that influence HRD in Southeast Asia. Regional HRD in Southeast Asia is a work in progress. As Severino (2015) points out, even the words used throughout the ASEAN blueprints talk of building, promoting, encouraging, increasing, improving, supporting. These gerunds demonstrate the ongoing nature of becoming and emergence. As ASEAN and the 11 countries of Southeast Asia continue to express their desire to be people-centric and make investments in the development of their people and communities, Regional HRD has an immense potential to positively influence the lives of all Southeast Asians.

Bibliography

Anderson, L. (2006). Analytic autoethnography. *Journal of Contemporary Ethnography, 35*(4), 373–395. https://doi.org/10.1177/0891241605280449.

Andriesse, E. (2017). Regional disparities in the Philippines: Structural drivers and policy considerations. *Erdkunde, 71*(2), 97–100. https://doi.org/10.3112/erdkunde.2017.02.01.

Association of Southeast Asian Nations. (2001). *Preparing workers for changes in the labour market: The ASEAN experience*. The ASEAN Secretariat. www.asean.org.

Association of Southeast Asian Nations. (2012). *ASEAN Document Series 2010*. The ASEAN Secretariat.

Association of Southeast Asian Nations. (2015). *ASEAN strategic action plan for SME development 2016–2025*. The ASEAN Secretariat. https://asean.org/wp-content/uploads/2015/12/SAP-SMED-Final.pdf.

Association of Southeast Asian Nations. (2017). *Compendium on migrant workers' education and safe migration programmes*. The ASEAN Secretariat.

Association of Southeast Asian Nations. (2020a). *ASEAN statistical yearbook 2020*. The ASEAN Secretariat. https://www.aseanstats.org/wp-content/uploads/2020/12/ASYB_2020.pdf.

Association of Southeast Asian Nations. (2020b). *ASEAN sustainable development goals indicators baseline report 2020*. The ASEAN Secretariat. https://www.aseanstats.org/wp-content/uploads/2020/11/ASEAN-Sustainable-Development-Goals-Indicators-Baseline-Report-2020-web.pdf.

Association of Southeast Asian Nations. (2020c). *ASEAN declaration on human resources development for the changing world of work*. The ASEAN Secretariat. https://asean.org/storage/2020/06/ASEAN-Declaration-on-Human-Resources-Development-for-the-Changing-World-of-Work.pdf.

Association of Southeast Asian Nations. (2021). *Chairman's statement on the ASEAN leaders meeting*. The ASEAN Secretariat. https://asean.org/storage/Chairmans-Statement-on-ALM-Five-Point-Consensus-24-April-2021-FINAL-a-1.pdf.

Avolio, B. J., & Bass, B. M. (2004). *Multifactor leadership questionnaire*. Mind Garden.

Balakrishnan, K. (2017). The ASEAN way of making regionalism work beyond five decades: Processes, remodelling and transformation. *Malaysian Journal of International Relations, 5*(1), 18–28.

Buszynski, L. (2019). Challenges to Southeast Asian regionalism in 2018. In D. Singh & M. Cook (Eds.), *Southeast Asian affairs 2019* (pp. 3–20). ISEAS—Yusof Ishak Institute.

Carpenter, D., & McGillivray, M. (2013). Narrowing the development gap: Policy recommendations for ASEAN and development partners. In M. McGillivray & D. Carpenter (Eds.), *Narrowing the development gap in ASEAN: Drivers and policy options* (pp. 178–200). Routledge.

Chai, D. S., Jeong, S., Kim, J., Kim, S., & Hamlin, R. G. (2016). Perceived managerial and leadership effectiveness in a Korean context: An indigenous qualitative study. *Asia Pacific Journal of Management, 33*(3), 789–820.

Coghlan, A. T., Preskill, H., & Tzavaras Catsambas, T. (2003). An overview of appreciative inquiry in evaluation. *New Directions for Evaluation*, 100, 5–22. https://doi.org/10.1002/ev.96.

Cook, A. D. B. (2018). Siloes, synergies and prospects for humanitarian assistance and disaster relief in Southeast Asia. In A. Chong (Ed.), *International security in the Asia-Pacific* (pp. 357–375). Palgrave Macmillan.

Cook, M. (2018). Southeast Asia's developing divide. In G. Rozman & J. C. Liow (Eds.), *International relations and Asia's southern tier* (pp. 63–76). Palgrave Macmillan.

Crocco, O. S., & Grenier, R. S. (2021). Not all those who wander are lost: Critically reflective research for a new HRD landscape. *Advances in Developing Human Resources, 23*(1), 55–65. https://doi.org/10.1177/1523422320973425.

Crocco, O. S., Nguyen, L., & Tkachenko, O. (2021). Vietnam and regional human resource development in ASEAN. In H. T. Tran, T. T. Phuong, H. T. M. Van, & G. N. McLean (Eds.), *Human resource development in Vietnam: Research and practice* (pp. 97–117). Palgrave Macmillan. https://doi.org/10.1007/978-3-030-51533-1_4.

Crocco, O. S., & Tkachenko, O. (2020). Regional human resource development: The case of Southeast Asia and ASEAN. *Human Resource Development International*. https://doi.org/10.1080/13678868.2020.1858261

Cseh, M., & Crocco, O. S. (2020). Globalizing HRD academic practice: Developing a global mindset for teaching and research. *Advances in Developing Human Resources, 22*(1), 51–71.

Davies, S. E. (2019). *Containing contagion: The politics of disease outbreaks in Southeast Asia*. Johns Hopkins University Press.

Doloriert, C., & Sambrook, S. (2012). Organisational autoethnography. *Journal of Organizational Ethnography*, *1*(1), 83–95. https://doi.org/10.1108/20466741211220688.

Dung, L. T., & Hai, P. V. (2020). The effects of transformational leadership and job satisfaction on commitment to organisational change: A three-component model extension approach. *The South East Asian Journal of Management, 14*(1), 106–123. https://doi/org/https://doi.org/10.21002/seam.v14i1.11585.

Ellis, C., & Bochner, A. (2000). Autoethnography, personal narrative, reflexivity: Researcher as subject. In N. K. Denzin & Y. S. Lincoln (Eds.), *Handbook of qualitative research* (2nd ed., pp. 733–768). Sage.

Emmerson, D. K. (2007). Challenging ASEAN: A "topological" view. *Contemporary Southeast Asia, 29*(3), 424–446.

Emmerson, D. K. (Ed.). (2020). *The deer and the dragon: Southeast Asia and China in the 21st century.* Walter H. Shorenstein Asia-Pacific Research Center.

Engel, U., & Mattheis, F. (Eds.). (2020). *The finances of regional organizations in the Global South.* Routledge.

Freedom House. (n.d.). *Internet freedom scores*. https://freedomhouse.org/countries/freedom-world/scores.

Garavan, T. N., McCarthy, A., & Carbery, R. (2019). An ecosystems perspective on international human resource development: A meta-synthesis of the literature. *Human Resource Development Review, 18*(2), 248–288. https://doi.org/10.1177/1534484319828865.

Gerard, K. (2014). *ASEAN's engagement of civil society: Regulating dissent*. Palgrave Macmillan.

Hägerdal, H., & Berlie, J. A. (2018). Timor-Leste and ASEAN. In J. A. Berlie (Ed.), *East Timor's independence, Indonesia, and ASEAN* (pp. 91–112). Palgrave Macmillan.

Hamlin, R. G. (2004). In support of universalistic models of managerial and leadership effectiveness: Implications for HRD research and practice. *Human Resource Development Quarterly, 15*(2), 189–215.

Hamlin, R. G., & Patel, T. (2017). Perceived managerial and leadership effectiveness within higher education in France. *Studies in Higher Education, 42*(2), 292–314.

Hamlin, R. G., & Whitford, S. (2020). Perceived managerial and leadership effectiveness within the Canadian public sector. *Human Resource Development Quarterly, 31*(4), 423–448.

Hantrais, L. (1999). Contextualization in cross-national comparative research. *International Journal of Social Research Methodology, 2*(2), 93–108.

Ismail, M. D., & Alam, S. S. (2019). Innovativeness and competitive advantage among small and medium enterprise exporters: Evidence from emerging markets in South East Asia. *The South East Asian Journal of Management, 13*(1), 74–91. https://doi/org/https://doi.org/10.21002/seam.v13i1.9872.

Jones, L. (2012). *ASEAN, sovereignty and intervention in Southeast Asia.* Palgrave Macmillan.

Jones, D. M., & Smith, M. L. R. (2006). *ASEAN and East Asian international relations: Regional delusion.* Edward Elgar.

Kathiravelu, L., & Wong, G. (2019). Marginalized migrants and urbanization in Southeast Asia. In R. Padawangi (Ed.), *Routledge handbook of urbanization in Southeast Asia* (pp. 146–156). Routledge.

Kausikan, B. (2020, October 24). ASEAN may have to cut members if they continue to be led by an external member. *Mothership.* https://mothership.sg/2020/10/bilahari-asean-china/.

Kim, S., & McLean, G. N. (2012). Global talent management: Necessity, challenges, and the roles of HRD. *Advances in Developing Human Resources, 14*(4), 566–585. https://doi.org/10.1177/1523422312455610.

Krasner, S. D. (1999). *Sovereignty: Organized hypocrisy.* Princeton University Press.

Lai, A. Y., He, J. A., Tan, T. B., & Phua, K. H. (2009). A proposed ASEAN disaster response, training and logistic centre enhanging regional governance in disaster management. *Transitions Studies Review, 16*(2), 299–315. https://doi.org/10.1007/s11300-009-0068-z.

Lum, S. K. (2013). Evolving a common surgical curriculum for ASEAN nations with a public health approach. *ANZ Journal of Surgery, 83*(3), 118–121. https://doi.org/10.1111/ans.12055.

Natalegawa, M. (2018). *Does ASEAN matter?* ISEAS Publishing.

Maria, R. F. S. (2018, January 22). *ASEAN economic integration: Myth or reality.* Lee Kuan Yew School of Public Policy. https://www.youtube.com/watch?v=QD7TNPkeaRY.

Marquart, M., Berger, N., & Loan, P. (2004). *HRD in the age of globalization.* Basic Books.

Marsan, G. A., & Sey, A. (2021). *Women's participation in the digital economy: Improving access to skills, entrepreneurship, and leadership across ASEAN.* Economic Research Institute for ASEAN and East Asia. https://www.eria.org/uploads/media/policy-brief/Women's-Participation-in-the-Digital-Economy_1203.pdf.

McGillivray, M., Feeny, S., & Iamsiraroj, S. (2013). Understanding the ASEAN development gap. In M. McGillivray & D. Carptenter (Eds.), *Narrowing the development gap in ASEAN: Drivers and policy options* (pp. 21–64). Routledge.

McLean, G. N. (2010). Human resource development scholar as rebel. *Human Resource Development Quarterly, 21*, 317–320. https://doi.org/10.1002/hrdq.20056.

McLean, G. N., Lynham, S. A., Azevedo, R. E., Lawrence, J. E., & Nafukho, F. M. (2008). A response to Wang and Swanson's article on National HRD and theory development. *Human Resource Development Review, 7*(2), 241–258. https://doi.org/10.1177/1534484308316486.

Pangestu, M. (2019, July 26). *Digital economy and development: An ASEAN perspective* [Video]. YouTube. https://www.youtube.com/watch?v=gjrx89sKpRA.

Parry, J., & Hayden, M. (2015). Skills development: A review with reference to Southeast Asia. *Journal of International and Comparative Education, 4*(2), 67–78. https://doi.org/10.14425/00.87.94.

Pruetipibultham, O. (2019). *Cultural adjustment for working and living in the Mekong Sub-region countries (Cambodia, Lao PDR, Myanmar, Vietnam)* [การปรับตัวในวัฒนธรรมลุ่มน้ำโขง CLMV (กัมพูชา สปป.ลาว เมียนมาร์และเวียดนาม)](in Thai). National Institute of Development Administration Publishing.

Puutio, T. A. (2016). Regional integration and the creative economies of ASEAN: Assessing the potential for a single ASEAN creative economy. In B. Jetin & M. Mikic (Eds.), *ASEAN economic community: A model for Asia-wide regional integration?* (pp. 231–240). Palgrave Macmillan.

Ra, S., Shrestha, U., Khatiwada, S., Yoon, S. W., & Kwon, K. (2019). The rise of technology and impact on skills. *International Journal of Training Research, 17*(1), 26–40. https://doi.org/10.1080/14480220.2019.1629727.

Roberts, C. (2010). *ASEAN's Myanmar crisis: Challenges to the pursuit of a security community.* Institute of Southeast Asian Studies.

Ruiz, C. E., Hamlin, R. G., & Esparza Martinez, L. (2014). Managerial and leadership effectiveness as perceived by managers and non-managerial employees in Mexico. *Human Resource Development International, 17*(3), 258–276.

Sakamoto, A. (2019). Reconceptualizing skills development for achieving inclusive growth: The horizon of a new generation of skills policy. *International Journal of Training Research, 17*(1), 69–82. https://doi.org/10.1080/14480220.2019.1632566.

Sale, J. (2020). Harmonisation of labour laws: An arduous journey for ASEAN. *Labour & Industry, 30*(1), 34–65.

Severino, R. C. (2015). From political/security concerns to regional economic integration. In O. K. Beng, S. B. Das, T. Chong, M. Cook, C. Lee, & M. Yeo (Eds.), *The 3rd ASEAN reader* (pp. 17–22). ISEAS Publishing.

Short, H. J., & Gray, D. E. (2018). HRD in SMEs: A research agenda whose time has come. *Human Resource Development Quarterly, 29*(1), 7–13. https://doi.org/10.1002/hrdq.21305.

Somkram, N. (2017). Online course design for creativity and innovative skills in virtual cultural ASEAN Community. *International Journal of Emerging Technologies in Learning, 12*(4), 4–20. https://doi.org/10.3991/ijet.v12i01.6032.

Stanton, P., & Nankervis, A. (2011). Linking strategic HRM, performance management and organizational effectiveness: Perceptions of managers in Singapore. *Asia Pacific Business Review, 17*(1), 67–84. https://doi.org/10.1080/13602381003790382.

Steiner, F. R. (2016). *Human ecology: How nature and culture shape our world.* Island Press.

Than, M. (2005). *Myanmar in ASEAN: Regional cooperation experience.* Institute of Southeast Asian Studies.

Tran, H. T., Phuong, T. T., Van, H. T. M., & McLean, G. N. (Eds.). (2021). *Human resource development in Vietnam: Research and practice.* Springer Nature.

Tubakovic, T. (2019). The failure of refugee protection and responsibility sharing: Policy neglect in the EU and ASEAN. *Asian and Pacific Migration Journal, 28*(2), 183–209. https://doi.org/10.1177/0117196819841094.

Turner, S. (2018). Ethnic minorities, indigenous groups and development tensions. In A. McGregor, L. Law, & F. Miller (Eds.), *Routledge handbook of Southeast Asian development* (pp. 224–237). Routledge.

Wang, G. G. (2008). National HRD: A new paradigm or the reinvention of the wheel? *Journal of European Industrial Training, 32*(4), 303–316. https://doi.org/10.1108/03090590810871397.

Wang, G. G., & Swanson, R. A. (2008). The idea of national HRD: An analysis based on economics and theory development methodology. *Human Resource Development Review, 7*(1), 79–106. https://doi.org/10.1177/1534484307311415.

Wang, G. G., Werner, M. J., Sun, J. Y., Gilley, W. J., & Gilley, A. (2017). Means versus ends: Theorizing a definition of human resource development. *Personnel Review, 46*(6), 1165–1181. https://doi.org/10.1108/PR-11-2015-0306.

Weatherbee, D. E. (2019). *ASEAN's half century: A political history of the Association of Southeast Asian Nations.* Rowman & Littlefield.

Zhu, C. J., & Warner, M. (2019). The emergence of human resource management in China: Convergence, divergence and contextualization. *Human Resource Management Review, 29*, 87–97. https://doi.org/10.1016/j.hrmr.2017.11.002.

Index

O. S. Crocco, *Developing Human Resources in Southeast Asia*, Palgrave Macmillan Asian Business Series, https://doi.org/10.1007/978-3-030-79697-6

The manufacturer's authorised representative in the EU is Springer Nature Customer Service Centre GmbH, Europaplatz 3, 69115 Heidelberg, Germany. If you have any concerns regarding our products, please contact ProductSafety@springernature.com

Printed and bound by CPI Group (UK) Ltd, Croydon, CR0 4YY
22/09/2026
02221054-0001